The Future of Marketing

The Future of Marketing

Critical 21st-Century Perspectives

Edited by

Philip J. Kitchen

First published 2003 by
PALGRAVE MACMILLAN
Houndmills, Basingstoke, Hampshire RG21 6XS and
175 Fifth Avenue, New York, N.Y. 10010
Companies and representative throughout the world

PALGRAVE MACMILLAN is the global academic imprint of the Palgrave Macmillan division of St. Martin's Press, LLC and of Palgrave Macmillan Ltd. Macmillan® is a registered trademark in the United States, United Kingdom and other countries. Palgrave is a registered trademark in the European Union and other countries.

ISBN 0–333–99286–5

This book is printed on paper suitable for recycling and made from fully managed and sustained forest sources.

A catalogue record for this book is available from the British Library.

Library of Congress Cataloging-in-Publication Data
The future of marketing: critical 21st-century perspectives/edited by Philip J. Kitchen.
    p. cm.
Includes bibliographical references and index.
ISBN 0–333–99286–5
    1. Marketing—Forecasting. 2. Twenty-first century—Forecasts.
I. Kitchen, Philip J.
HF5415.F945 2003
658.8'001 12–dc21   2002029402

10   9   8   7   6   5   4   3   2   1
12   11   10   09   08   07   06   05   04   03

Printed and bound in Great Britain by
Antony Rowe Ltd, Chippenham and Eastbourne

*To my wife Diane for her continued help, support
and happy companionship*

Contents

List of figures

List of tables

Notes on the contributors

Professor Philip J. Kitchen, The Business School, University of Hull, Hull, UK HU6 7RX. Tel: +44 (0) 1482 466349; Fax: +44 (0) 1482 346311; Email: p.j.kitchen@hull.ac.uk

Philip J. Kitchen, the editor of this book and author of Chapters 1, 10 and 11 holds the Chair in Strategic Marketing at Hull University Business School, Hull University, UK. Prior to this he held the Martin Naughton Chair in Business Strategy, specializing in Marketing, at Queen's University, Belfast where he founded and directed the Executive MBA programme. At Hull, he teaches and carries out research in marketing management, marketing communications, corporate communications, promotion management and international communications manage-ment, and has a specific aim of building an active team of marketing researchers. Before Queen's he was Senior Lecturer in Marketing and Founder and Director of the Research Centre for Corporate and Marketing Communications within the Department of Marketing at Strathclyde University. A graduate of the CNAA (BA[Hons]) initially, he received Masters degrees in Marketing from UMIST (MSc) and Manchester Business School (MBSc) respectively, and his PhD from Keele University. Since 1984 he has been active in teaching and research in the communications domain. He is Founding Editor and now Editor-in-Chief of the *Journal of Marketing Communications* (Routledge Journals, 1995). He has published five books so far, including: *Public Relations: Principles and Practice* (International Thomson, 1997), *and Marketing Communications: Principles and Practice* (1999); *Communicating Globally: An Integrated Marketing Approach* (2000), and *Raising the Corporate Umbrella: Corporate Communications in the 21st Century* (2001), both with Don Schultz of Northwestern University (NTC Business Books, Chicago, and Palgrave, Basingstoke). He was co-editor of *Marketing: The Informed Student Guide* (2000), with Tony Proctor (International Thomson).

Dr Kitchen has contributed to such journals as the *Journal of Advertising Research, Journal of Business Ethics, International Journal of Market Research, International Journal of Advertising, Journal of Marketing Management, European Journal of Marketing, Marketing Intelligence and Planning, Journal of Marketing Communications, ADMAP, Journal of Nonprofit and Public Sector Marketing, International Journal of Bank Marketing, Journal of Corporate Communications, Small Business and Enterprise Development, Creativity and Innovation Management*; and numerous practitioner journals. Dr Kitchen founded, organized, and chaired the 1st International Conference on Marketing and Corporate Communications and was Editor of the Proceedings (Keele, 1996; Strathclyde, 1998). This Conference is now an annual event (Antwerp, Belgium, 1997; Glasgow, Scotland, 1998; Salford, England, 1999; Erasmus Universiteit, the Netherlands, 2000; Queen's, 2001; Antwerp, 2002). Dr Kitchen serves on the Editorial Advisory Board of the *Journal of Marketing Management* and is a Review Board Member for *Marketing Intelligence and Planning and Corporate Communications: An International Journal*. He holds Visiting Chair appointments at Massey University, New Zealand, and the School of Management, Rouen University, France.

He has given papers on marketing management, corporate or marketing communications in England, Scotland, the Czech Republic, Estonia, France, Germany, Belgium, Portugal, Australia, New Zealand, Spain, the Republic of Ireland, Northern Ireland, Israel, the Netherlands and in the United States.

He is also active in the professional arena. He is a member of the Measurement Academic Advisory Panel (MAAP) with Hill & Knowlton, Inc. which involves leading academics from Europe, Pacific Rim, and America. This group seeks to bring a robust academic dimension to Hill & Knowlton thinking across a wide range of measurement evaluation tools.

Professor Don E. Schultz, Medill School of Journalism, Northwestern University, 1908 Sheridan Road, Evanston, IL 60208-1290, USA. Tel: +1 847 491 5665; Fax: +1 847 491 5925; Email: dschultz@lulu.acns. nwu.edu

Don E. Schultz, author of Chapter 2, is Professor (Emeritus) of Integrated Marketing Communications (IMC) at the Medill School of

Journalism, Northwestern University, Evanston, IL, USA. Professor Schultz and his colleagues pioneered the first graduate programme in IMC. He is also President of his own marketing communication and management firm: Agora, Inc., in Evanston, IL. Professor Schultz has consulted, lectured, and held seminars in marketing, marketing metrics, marketing communication, branding, advertising, sales promotion, and other topics in North and South America, Europe, the Middle East, Australia, New Zealand and Asia. He was Founding Editor of the *Journal of Direct Marketing*, and has published eleven books including *Integrated Marketing Communications* (1992) which he co-authored with Stanley Tannenbaum and Robert Lauterborn. His landmark text, *Measuring Brand Communication ROI*, written with Jeffrey Walters, has revolutionized the entire field of marketing communication and branding measurement.

Professor Schultz is a prolific writer. He has published over 100 articles, research papers, and studies in scholarly journals around the world. He is a regular columnist for *Marketing News* and *Marketing Management*, both published by the American Marketing Association. He is on the editorial board of half a dozen scholarly journals published around the world.

Professor W. Fred van Raaij, Faculty of Social and Behavioural Sciences, Katholieke Universiteit Brabant, Warandelaan 2, PO Box 90153, 5000 Le Tilburg, The Netherlands. Tel: +31 (0) 13 466 2434; Fax: +31 (0) 13 466 2067; Email: W.F. vanRaaij@kub.nl

W. Fred van Raaij, co-author of Chapter 3, has been Professor of Economic Psychology at Tilburg University since 2000 and is also chairman of the GVR, Centre for Marketing Communication, Amsterdam. He was Professor of Economic Psychology at the Department of Economics (1979–93) and Professor of Marketing at the Department of Management (1993–2000) of Erasmus University, Rotterdam. He has published many articles and papers in scientific journals and conference proceedings, and written several books on consumer behaviour and marketing communication. His main interests concern the use of new media such as the Internet, marketing communication, behavioural economics and behavioural finance. This chapter also shows his interest in trends and the future of marketing.

Professor Dr Theo B.C. Poiesz, Economic Psychology, Department of Social Sciences, Tilburg University, P803 PO Box 90153, 5000 Le Tilburg, The Netherlands. Tel: +31 (0) 13 4663203; Email: t.b.c.poiesz@kub.nl

Theo Poiesz, co-author of Chapter 3, has been Professor of Economic Psychology at the Tilburg University since 1992 and is also academic director of the Marketing College, Tias Business School. He was Professor of the Psychology of Advertising at Tilburg University (1988–92; part-time), and Professor of Marketing at the University of Maastricht (1989–92; part-time). He has published many articles and papers in academic journals, professional journals and conference proceedings, and written several books. His main research interests concern the interface between marketing and psychology, the effectiveness of communication, behaviour management (the application of psychological insights in practical settings), and supplier–customer relationships. A recent interest concerns the future of marketing.

Professor Walter van Waterschoot, Universiteit of Antwerp, Faculty of Applied Economics (RUCA), Department of Marketing, Prinstraat 13 – 2000, Antwerpen, Belgium. Tel: +32 3 220 41 1; Fax: 32 3 220 47 99; Email: walter.vanwaterschoot@ua.ac.be

Walter van Waterschoot, co-author of Chapter 4, is Professor of Marketing at the University of Antwerp (Belgium). He is a regular marketing textbook author. His main marketing textbook (written in Dutch) is currently in its ninth edition. He has also contributed to many international textbooks, including *The Oxford Textbook of Marketing*, *The Encyclopedia of Marketing* and *The International Encyclopedia of Business and Management*. He has co-authored articles in authoritative journals such as the *Journal of Marketing* and the *Journal of Retailing*. He is also active in academic marketing consultancy, with assignments from leading companies such as Alfa Laval, Dupont de Nemours, Gedas Automation Systems, Douwe Egberts (Sara Lee), Bekaert Textiles and Janssen-Cilag (Johnson & Johnson).

Professor Els Gilbrecht, University of Tilburg, Faculty of Economics, Department of Marketing, Warandeburg 2, PO Box 90153, 5000 Le Tilburg. Tel: +31 (0) 13 466 82 24; Fax: +31 (0) 13 466 28 75; Email: e.gilbrecht@kub.nl

Els Gilbrecht, co-author of Chapter 4, is Professor of Marketing at the University of Tilburg (the Netherlands). She is a regular academic marketing researcher. She is active in several international research organizations and networks such as the Marketing Science Institute, and the European Marketing Academy. Her articles have appeared in authoritative journals such as the *International Journal of Research in Marketing*, and the *Journal of Retailing*. In addition, she has contributed to many international textbooks, including *The Oxford Textbook of Marketing*, *The Encyclopedia of Marketing* and *Research Traditions in Marketing*. She is also active in academic marketing consultancy, with assignments from leading companies: Gfk, Bekaert Textiles, Janssen-Cilag (Johnson & Johnson), Mazda, Procter & Gamble and the GIB group.

Professor Michael Thomas, Department of Marketing, Strathclyde University, Stenhouse Building, 173 Cathedral Street, Glasgow G4 0RQ. Tel: 0141 552 4400; Email: Michael.Thomas@Mi8.com

Michael Thomas, OBE, OM Poland, author of Chapter 5, is an Emeritus Professor of Marketing at Strathclyde University, Scotland. He is President of the Marketing Research Society, and a Chartered Marketer. He was Chairman of The Chartered Institute of Marketing, 1995. He is the editor of *Marketing Intelligence and Planning* which is now in its twentieth volume. He is the author of twelve books, the most recent of which are *The Handbook of Strategic Marketing* (1998) and *International Marketing* (1998), and has published numerous chapters in books and many articles in learned journals around the world. He is (or has been) Visiting Professor at Georgetown University, Syracuse University, University of Tennessee, University of Malta, Helsinki School of Economics, Linkoping University, Karlstad University, Gdansk Management Training Foundation, Warsaw International Management School, University of Novy Sancz, Lincoln School of Management, DeMontfort University and Birmingham University.

Professor John Philip Jones, Newhouse School of Public Communications, Syracuse University, New York, USA (please write to him at 122 Edgehill Road, Syracuse, NY 13224, USA)

John Philip Jones, the author of Chapter 6, is a British-born American academic. He spent 27 years in the advertising business, working mainly for J. Walter Thompson. He has been for more than 20 years at the Newhouse School of Public Communications, Syracuse University, New York. He is tenured full professor of the advertising department and was for seven years chairman of that department. He is also an adjunct professor at the Royal Melbourne Institute of Technology, Australia, which he visits every year.

He is the author of five books on advertising, and editor and part-author of five others. He has been responsible for about 100 articles which have appeared in professional academic and general publications.

He addresses professional conferences and carries out much outside consultancy. In connection with this work he does a large amount of international travel every year.

Professor Cees van Riel, Director – Corporate Communication Centre, Rotterdam School of Management, Erasmus University, Rotterdam, The Netherlands; Email: criel@fbk.eur.nl

Cees van Riel, co-author of Chapter 7, is Professor of Corporate Communications and Director of the Corporate Communications Centre at the Rotterdam School of Management, Erasmus University, Rotterdam. He is also European Director of the Reputation Institute. He has published numerous papers in such journals as *Management Communication Quarterly* and *Public Relations Review*. His book, *Principles of Corporate Communications*, was published by Prentice-Hall International in 1995 and was followed by other monographs. He is one of the Founding Editors of the international journal *Corporate Reputation Review*.

Guido Berens, Erasmus Research Institute of Management, Erasmus University, Rotterdam, The Netherlands

Guido Berens, co-author of Chapter 7, is close to completing his doctoral degree at the Erasmus Research Institute of Management of Erasmus University, Rotterdam, the Netherlands. His research focuses on the influence of corporate reputation on companies' relationships with stakeholders. His background is in cognitive psychology.

Professor Stephen Brown, Professor of Marketing Research, Faculty of Business and Management, University of Ulster, Newtownabbey, County Antrim, Northern Ireland BT37 0QB. Tel: +44 028 9036 6130; Fax: +44 028 9036 6868; Email: sjbrown@adt.co.uk

Stephen Brown, author of Chapter 8, is Professor of Marketing Research at the University of Ulster, UK. He has written numerous books, including *Postmodern Marketing*, *Songs of the Humpback Shopper*, and *Marketing: The Retro Revolution*. His articles have been published in *Harvard Business Review*, *Business Horizons*, *Journal of Advertising*, *Journal of Retailing*, and many others. He has been a Visiting Professor at Northwestern University, the University of Utah, and the University of California (Irvine) and others. Additional information is available from the website www.sfxbrown.com.

Professor Jagdish (Jag) N. Sheth, 1549 Clairmont Road, Suite 203, Decatur, GA 30033 Tel: 404-325-0757 (office); 404-325-0313 (home office); Fax: 404-325-1313 (fax); Email: jag@jagsheth.com

Jagdish (Jag) N. Sheth, co-author of Chapter 9, is the Charles H. Kellstadt Professor of Marketing in the Goizueta Business School and the founder of the Center for Relationship Marketing at Emory University. Prior to his present position, he was at the University of Southern California (7 years) and the founder of the Centre for Telecommunications Management (CTM); at the University of Illinois (15 years), and on the faculty of Columbia University (5 years), as well as the Massachusetts Institute of Technology (2 years). Dr Sheth is nationally and internationally known for his scholarly contribution in Marketing, Customer Satisfaction, Global Competition, and Strategic Thinking.

Professor Sheth has worked for numerous industries and companies in the United States, Europe and Asia, both as an adviser and as a seminar leader. His clients include AT&T, BellSouth, Cox Communications, Delta, Ernst & Young, Ford, GE, Lucent Technologies, Motorola, Nortel, Pillsbury, Sprint, Square D, 3M, Whirlpool and many more. He has offered more than 5,000 presentations in at least 20 countries. He is also on the Board of Directors of several public companies including Norstan (NASDAQ) and Wipro Limited (NYSE).

In 1989, Dr Sheth was given the Outstanding Marketing Educator award by the Academy of Marketing Science. In 1991, and again in 1999, he was given the Outstanding Educator Award by the Sales and Marketing Executives International (SMEI). Dr Sheth was also awarded the P.D. Converse Award for his outstanding contributions to theory in marketing in 1992 by the American Marketing Association. In 1996, Dr Sheth was selected as the Distinguished Fellow of the Academy of Marketing Science. In 1997, Dr Sheth was awarded the Distinguished Fellow award from the International Engineering Consortium. Dr Sheth is also a Fellow of the American Psychological Association (APA).

In 1999, Dr Sheth co-authored a textbook with Banwari Mittal, *Customer Behavior: Consumer Behavior and Beyond*. In 2000, Dr Sheth and Andew Sobel published a best seller, *Clients for Life* (Simon & Schuster) and in 2001, the book *Value Space* (McGraw-Hill), co-authored with Banwari Mittal, was published. Look for his latest book, *The Rule of Three* (Free Press), co-authored with Rajendra Sisodia.

Professor Rajendra S. Sisodia, Department of Marketing, Bentley College, 175 Forest Street, Waltham, MA 02154. Tel: 781-891-3461 (office); Fax: 781-891-3410; Email: rsisodia@bentley.edu

Rajendra S. Sisodia, co-author of Chapter 9, is Trustee Professor of Marketing and Founding Director of the Center for Marketing Technology at Bentley College. Previously, he was Director of executive Programs and Associate Professor of Marketing at George Mason University (GMU) in Fairfax, Virginia. His responsibilities there included directing the Executive MBA programme, the Masters programme in Technology Management and short executive programmes. Before joining GMU, he was Assistant Professor of Marketing at Boston University. An electrical engineer by undergraduate training, Dr Sisodia has a PhD in Marketing and Business Policy from Columbia University.

Dr Sisodia's book, *The Rule of Three: How Competition Shapes Markets* (with Jagdish N. Sheth) was published by the Free Press division of Simon & Schuster in 2002. In addition, Dr Sisodia has published approximately 70 articles in varied publications, including *Harvard Business Review, Journal of Business Strategy, Journal of Business Research, Journal of the Academy of Marketing Science, Handbook of Business Strategy, Marketing Letters, Marketing Management, Marketing Research, Journal of Services Marketing, Routledge Encyclopedia of Marketing, American Marketing Association Marketing Encyclopedia, Information and Management, Telecommunications Policy, International Journal of Technology Management, Design Management Journal, Personal Computers and Artificial Intelligence, Journal of Global Business* and *Journal of Professional Services Marketing*. He has authored several book chapters and about two dozen marketing cases.

Dr Sisodia is listed in *Who's Who in America* and *Who's Who in Finance and Industry*. He writes frequently for many leading newspapers and business magazines including the *Wall Street Journal* and *Fortune*.

Acknowledgements

The editor and publishers wish to thank the outstanding group of contributors for sharing their knowledge, expertise, understanding and experience with the readers of this book. This bringing together of a group of world-class professors to share their critical perspectives on marketing and its future is probably without parallel. I am indebted to the contributors who helped clarify the context for this book. Their expertise and co-operation has been invaluable.

I acknowledge, with the contributors, the various individuals, companies, and research journals that have assisted us by allowing material to be cited and shared. Also, we thank the many myriads of marketing students who through their questions and comments have helped the authors sharpen and hone their critical faculties. And we must also acknowledge the literally thousands of practitioners and colleagues who, through workshops, seminars, conferences and symposia, have influenced development of the thoughts expressed in this book.

To all of you, thank you for your help, guidance, support and encouragement as we offer these critical perspectives on the discipline of marketing, what it is, and what it may yet become, as we move forward into the 21st century.

PHILIP J. KITCHEN

Every effort has been made to trace all copyright-holders of material used in this book, but if any have been inadvertently overlooked the publishers will be pleased to make the necessary arrangement at the first opportunity.

List of abbreviations

CAPs	Company Advertising Policies
CCO	Chief Customer Officer
CEO	Chief Executive Officer
COO	Chief Operating Officer
CRM	Customer Relationship Management
EPS	Extensive Problem Solving
ERP	Enterprise Resource Planning
fmcg	fast-moving consumer goods
ICT	Information and Communication Technology
IT	Information Technology
LPS	Limited Problem Solving
MMM	Marketing Mix Modelling
NPD	New Product Development
P&L	Profit and Loss
PLC	Product Life Cycle
ROI	Return on Investment
RRB	Routinised Response Behaviour
TQM	Total Quality Management

Editorial stance on the future of marketing: critical 21st-century perspectives

philip j. kitchen

Aims

This book has been developed to suit the needs of practitioners and students who wish to develop an understanding of marketing from an international standpoint. It will provide a series of critical perspectives about marketing from senior authors around the world. The book is not about 'what marketing *is*' for this is already amply recorded in innumerable texts; rather, the book turns to leading authors and critics for their comments, views, positive statements, and criticisms and doubts concerning marketing and its role within business and as an academic subject in the 21st century.

Introduction

The book is designed to enable marketers and students to ponder more deeply the meaning of marketing, and how marketing might be applied in today's and tomorrow's world. It is for readers who wish to develop knowledge of, information about and insight into marketing. It is edited primarily because critical perspectives of marketing and its future require plurality of thought. As will be seen in the chapters, each of the senior academics chosen has developed a critical perspective of marketing from their specific contexts. Such perspectives cannot be derived purely from either a single author or from an external critic looking in, and thus the book draws various chapters from recognized experts. Unusually, each chapter is not proscribed into a particular subject topic, as the editor wished the contributors to 'speak for themselves'.

Is such a book really needed? Marketing as a subject area is riding high on the waves of public, economic and political opinion in the world. The concepts of 'the market', 'market forces', 'marketing management', 'global marketing' and 'marketing warfare' are common parlance. But there are also nagging concerns about marketing, especially in the multinational/global arena, to the effect that perhaps the topic of marketing or the behaviour of firms adopting the concept are open to question, perhaps even criticism. A further concern is that marketing itself may be a metaphor – and perhaps even a poor one – underlying deeper exchange relationships that have to be conceptualized more appropriately. A further point seems to be that, despite an ever-increasing crescendo of firms adopting the marketing concept, there is a growing unease among customers and consumers. Are needs really being satisfied? Is marketing more to do with competitive focus than consumer focus? Is marketing more concerned with rhetoric, spin and jargon than actually seeking to satisfy customer needs? Thus the book, among other things, raises critical theoretical questions, citing issues of current and emergent importance among marketing thinkers.

Is this book for you?

Do you belong in any of the following categories?

- A practitioner in marketing: marketing executive, marketing manager, brand manager, market researcher, or in any field associated with marketing as practice
- Associated with a professional organization such as the Chartered Institute of Marketing (UK), the American Marketing Association, or other professional marketing associations around the world
- An undergraduate student studying for a degree in marketing or on a course of study where marketing plays a prominent role
- A marketing academic
- A postgraduate student studying for a direct qualification in marketing (MA, MPhil, MSc) or on a course where marketing is offered as an integral component (i.e., MBA) or as a specialist stream (MA, MPhil, MSc)

■ A doctoral student in any of the domains of marketing

■ Or are you concerned about what marketing is now, what it claims to be, or where marketing is going in the future?

If the answer is 'yes' to any of the above then this book is a 'must read' for you.

Genesis of the book

The origins of any book, even one that is edited, lie in some spark of creativity. In this case, my thinking on the subject of marketing was stimulated by:

(a)   direct involvement as a teacher and researcher in the domain of marketing for nearly two decades;

(b)   continuous reading in the subject area (the attempt to understand what marketing is, where it has come from, where it stands now as a theoretical and practical discipline, and how and in what ways it may develop in the future);

(c)   association with many colleagues and students who have stimulated me by their company, and their critical comments, amid the ongoing whirl of academic activity in the marketing discipline, (if their names were to be recorded for posterity this would almost form a chapter in its own right).

In particular five books have been of specific resonance as this edited text has unfolded. These were by Bartels (1962); Cox, Alderson and Shapiro (1964); Sheth, Gardner and Garrett (1988); Hunt (1991) and Baker (1999). These books are cited here in chronological order, though I have accessed them at different times and for different reasons. Most readers and thinkers in marketing will be familiar with them.

Robert Bartels (1962), *The Development of Marketing Thought*

This book traces the history of marketing thought from 1900 until 1960:

(a)   1900–10 *Period of Discovery*
(b)   1910–20 *Period of Conceptualization*

(c)   1920–30 *Period of Integration*
(d)   1930–40 *Period of Development*
(e)   1940–50 *Period of Reappraisal*
(f)   1950–60 *Period of Reconception*

It is interesting to note that Theodore Levitt's (1960) milestone article, 'Marketing Myopia', which has had such a profound impact on the development of marketing, was actually published two years before Bartels' book, thus fitting very neatly into his conceptual framework. I regard Bartels' book as a critical milestone charting the first 60 years of marketing development and thought.

Reavis Cox, Wroe Alderson and Stanley Shapiro (eds) (1964), *Theory in Marketing*

Just two years after the Bartels text, Cox, Alderson and Shapiro edited the second series text on behalf of the American Marketing Association, titled *Theory in Marketing Systems*. Here, a specific and formative influence was exerted on my thinking by the contribution titled 'A Normative Theory of Marketing systems' by Wroe Alderson, where he likens firms to biological entities (product life cycle theorists like these), and from which I quote:

> The best analogy for the capacity of a system to survive is the health of a biological organism ... it is rational to exercise proper care to keep the body or the system healthy. The prime strategy is a ... strategy of avoidance. The individual tries to avoid infection or other conditions that might cause illness. Through occasional medical examinations he hopes for early detection of what might otherwise be become an incurable and otherwise fatal disease. The executive watches for maladjustment in the system and attempts to provide prompt remedies. *Above all, he should try to prevent the system from falling into the condition that has been called the extinction mode.* (Alderson, 1964; italics added)

Marketing itself can be seen as a system with sets of rules, norms, values, definitions, models and approaches. In this book, several authors identify serious health problems with the system known as marketing. One author, Thomas, states that the marketing profession, at least in its academic ranks, is suffering from *epistemopathology* or the application of: 'diseased, sick, and bad knowledge that is mechanistically applied to contemporary global market systems, in self serving ways, to identify and solve immediate problems, problems which are not well understood, and without any consideration of the ripple effects on society as a whole'. Evidently, parts of marketing may be ill or diseased, and may be in need of remedial attention. Among other things, therefore, this book is a clarion call to all involved with the discipline – either practically or as teachers – to understand the conceptual rock on which they are founded, and to help strengthen and indeed renew the foundations.

Jagdish Sheth, David Gardner and Dennis Garrett (1988), *Marketing Theory: Evolution and Evaluation*

Some 20 years later, and without full or even partial justice to all the books and articles in between (see Arndt, 1976; Bartels, 1983; Day and Wensley, 1983; Hunt, 1983, 1992; Dholakia and Arndt, 1985; Firat, Dholakia and Bagozzi, 1987; Fullerton, 1987; Shapiro and Walle, 1987; Zinkhan and Hirscheim, 1992, for example), in this idiosyncratic review Jagdish Sheth, David Gardner, and Dennis Garrett's book, started to reveal – at least to me – some startling deficiencies between what was then taught to undergraduate and postgraduate students and what was actually known about the subject.

The book attempted to 'describe all the major schools of thought that had arisen in marketing since its emergence as an independent discipline in the early 1900's'. Sheth, Gardner and Garrett's typology included the following:

1 Noninteractive-economic schools of marketing including:
   (a)   commodity school;
   (b)   functional school;
   (c)   regional school.

2 Interactive-economic schools of marketing including:
   (a)   institutional school;
   (b)   functionalist school;
   (c)   managerial school.

3 Noninteractive-noneconomic schools of marketing including:
   (a)   buyer behaviour school;
   (b)   macromarketing school;
   (c)   activist school.

4 Interactive-noneconomic schools of marketing including:
   (a)   organizational dynamics school;
   (b)   systems school;
   (c)   social exchange school.

For marketers, irrespective of whether they practise marketing or teach it to others, this book is a very useful introduction to 12 schools of marketing thought of which they may only have been taught one specific school, without necessarily giving thought to any of the others. It is a useful exercise to see inside which school of thought a marketing practitioner or academic may have received their initial training. Certainly now the managerial school and the buyer behaviour school appear to have arrived at a position of dominance in terms of contributing answers to the question of what marketing is, and where it is going in the future.

The following question was of interest to me in 1988 and is still of interest today, especially in the context of this book; Sheth, Gardner and Garrett also indicated that marketing was facing two major problems:

The question:
Why should marketing scholars even endeavour to develop a general theory of marketing?

The problems:
Marketing was (and is) undergoing an identity crisis. In 1998 the question 'what is marketing?' drew the response: 'The fact is, we currently are not very sure just what marketing is and what it should be.'

In addition to an identity crisis, marketing was (and is) also experiencing a credibility crisis. Marketing practitioners were (and are) becoming increasingly disillusioned with the advice offered by their academic counterparts.

Shelby D. Hunt (1991), *Modern Marketing Theory*

Some three years later, Shelby Hunt's (1991) monograph, *Modern Marketing Theory: Critical Issues in the Philosophy of Marketing Science*, started to ask some telling and searching questions in relation to the marketing discipline. Some of these questions have significance in the current context.

1   How does one scientifically explain marketing phenomena?
2   Can one understand marketing phenomena without being able to explain or predict them?
3   What is the role of laws and lawlike generalizations in marketing [research]?
4   How can marketing phenomena best be classified?

Now, admittedly, Hunt's monograph is an attempt to assert that 'the study of marketing theory is the most *practical* intellectual pursuit of anyone seriously interested in marketing research' (p. 1). However, here I see the questions as being relevant to practitioners and academics concerned with the business of marketing either in practical or theoretical terms. Thus one way to depict '*the future of marketing*' is to understand where it has come from and where it stands now, but that requires a critical insight. Here, too, Hunt provides a critical insight for our discipline:

> consistent with Western philosophical thought since the Enlightenment, human agency contends that society is now and can be in the future what people make of it, that is, that people can 'make a difference'. *So it is in marketing. Nothing is inexorable in the marketing discipline*: not reification, intellectualisation, quantitative methods, qualitative methods, positivism, realism, failure, success, nor I might add, our very survival. (p. 443)

Hunt concludes his book by citing from one of his own pages (Hunt, 1989), when he says: 'Perhaps because of marketing's youth, our literature has never developed a critical tradition.' He then calls for a more critical approach, saying: 'Isn't the goal of disciplinary advancement worth maximum effort on all our parts?'

Michael Baker (ed.) (1999), *Encyclopaedia of Marketing*

The final book that I have found of value in my search to understand what marketing means is by no means purely concerned with the theory of marketing. I refer to Michael Baker's (1999) epic *Encyclopaedia of Marketing*, which is a worthy reference text. While one could refer to any of the sections derived from academic marketing leaders, I would specifically recommend to readers the final chapter, titled 'The Future of Marketing', by the editor. Baker explores four fundamental topics:

- Where are we now?
- Alternative perspectives
- Evolution, not revolution
- The futures of marketing.

I particularly like his section entitled 'The futures of marketing'. This suggests a diversity and plurality of potential futures. He states:

> it is clear that managing the marketing function is more than enough to ensure marketing and marketers have a challenging future ahead of them. As to whether 'marketing' will be seen as the primary source of strategic thinking and business leadership *that must surely depend both on what marketers perceive it to be **and on what they do***. (p. 830) (italics and bold added)

Baker indicates that marketing does have a future. A future in terms of functions, yes: but what is the contribution to be made by those thinking and writing about the discipline?

Surely, it is time for marketers, whether practitioners or academics working at the coalface, to reconsider what marketing is now. That reconsideration can and will be reflected in the various journals, magazines and books that chart the progression of our discipline. The onus of what is done rests on the shoulders of the current generation of marketers, irrespective of whichever side of theory and practice they lie.

Obviously, the books and articles I have cited are selected arbitrarily. Other more erudite and insightful expositions of marketing will be found, and readers are encouraged to make their own path through the literature. I, among others, will wait to hear the outcomes.

Two final points regarding the genesis of this text: first, my own research deals predominantly with marketing and corporate communications, and is increasingly focused on the brand (either individual or corporate) as the unit of analysis. As a result of researching in both these areas, two books were published which – at least in my mind – had significant ramifications and resonance for the marketing discipline. The first of these books was Schultz and Kitchen (2000). In this text, the authors described a four-phase model by which 'integrated marketing communication' (IMC) – a means of developing and implementing measurable, persuasive, brand communication programmes – could be appropriated by national, international and global companies. Application of the model in its initial stage can be no more than fusing together of promotional mix elements, which is a typical inside-out approach to marketing. As we move through the phases of the model, however, to outside-in, to customer database building, and finally to strategic and financial integration where behavioural measurement becomes possible (see Chapters 4 and 11 of the text), we realized that what may have started in the promotional sphere has ramifications for the entire range of marketing activities. What a pity to discover therefore that so many organizations and businesses were reluctant to move past the very first stage, for driving a customer focus deeply into an organization requires significant analysis and adjustment of organizational structures, requires new mind sets and new behaviours by marketers, and also requires new ways of gathering information in order to build and sustain market, mind and heart shares. We concluded by suggesting that in order to build integrated communication globally, significant barriers had to be overcome. Note that these barriers are not just applicable to IMC, *but also to the marketing discipline in general*. Some of the book's conclusions are repeated below (Schultz and Kitchen, 2000):

1 The marketing world requires new developmental paths for marketers at all organizational levels.

2 Marketers must balance marketplaces with marketspaces.

3 Organizational constraints must be recognized as such, and overcome over time.

4 A research-rich consumer understanding is vital.

5 Both marketing communications *and* corporate communications are needed to effectively compete in today's crowded and turbulent environment.

6 Marketing training is required at *all* organizational levels.

7 Mind maps – ways of seeing the marketing world – may need to be revisited, re-viewed, and re-adjusted to reflect current developments.

One important range of criteria for marketing and marketers can be found in the interface between corporate and marketing communications. This led to the second book (this time edited), which focused on the need for the corporate brand: see Kitchen and Schultz (2001). The use of the umbrella metaphor was derived directly from an earlier book by Charles Handy, *The Empty Raincoat* (1995). What we meant by the metaphor was that senior executives, led by the Chief Executive Officer (CEO), need to conceive and present the corporation in such a way that it not only protects and nurtures all the strategic business units and individual brands within its portfolio, but that *the organization itself stands for more than an anonymous faceless profit-taking corporate entity*:

> Such an organisation and its total meaning, that is, its 'corporate umbrella', cannot be hoisted by empty corporate entities. The corporation can only be communicated

when its managers understand and practice a total integrated communication program that puts reality and realism inside the firm that can then be communicated to the various stakeholders and those who might have a relationship of some sort with the firm.

Thus the 'umbrella' acts as force-field metaphor in that it is like an umbrella in each of its structural aspects from handle (in the hands of a CEO), to ribs (the functions of corporate communication), to the cloth (which protects from the elements outside), to the ferrule (which acts as a data-gathering device). Of course, if the cloth is torn, or a rib broken (i.e., there is a failure to act or be perceived to act in a socially responsible manner), then the corporation is exposed to 'the slings and arrows of outrageous fortune'.

Again, a book that appeared to focus on one aspect of significant importance to all businesses and firms also has resonance for the marketing discipline.

The final strand of 'genesis' took place in 2001. Each year, the Academy of Marketing (UK) organizes a conference. For the first time, however, in 2001 the Marketing and Strategy Group at Cardiff University organized a 'research event', entitled 'In Search of Excellence for Research in Marketing'. The purpose of the event, which is now held annually, is to: 'examine effective ways of stimulating scholarly research in marketing of international excellence [within the UK]'. I personally found attendance at this event to be worthwhile. It served to stimulate the grey matter concerning what marketing is, and was, and where the discipline is going. For there is indeed a problem with marketing in the UK: despite all the teaching, writing, instruction and training given now over 30 or more years, so many firms are *bad at marketing*. More consumers and customers are provided with lower-quality products, with higher-than-average prices and with poorer services here in this country than in any other country I know. Virtually any comparison of any product category in this country compared to others (even if we just compare with the USA or another European nation) reveals significant shortcomings and a pronounced lack of ability to satisfy customer needs. So even as academics pronounce the virtues of an American-led marketing concept in lecture theatres, and as marketing managers polish their trappings of marketing, so the substance of marketing seems to escape attention.

Maybe this book is one, albeit small, attempt to address these issues.

The content: shaping the future

I have been pleased and delighted that so many learned and leading professors from the world of marketing have provided a contribution for this book. These professors from the USA, Europe, and the UK were invited arbitrarily by me to submit a chapter precisely because they were asking critical questions about marketing, or their research had ramifications for marketing, or their works implied changes had to be made in the discipline of marketing for the future. They, however, are not the only people speaking on and writing about these issues; behind these critics are potentially thousands of other people who have helped shape the world of marketing as we know it today. However, as will be seen within the chapters that follow, that world of *shaping* is still going on, both from this contribution and those that will follow.

Conclusion

This is a rather unusual introductory chapter. What I have to do now is get out of the way, in order to allow the authors to speak for themselves. Each provides a critical perspective on marketing; each refers – in one way or another – to the future of marketing. I prefer to think of these chapters as encountering individual minds, in process of reflection on our discipline. I hope that readers will enjoy the encounters as I have. As you now set out on their journey of discovery, I will be walking alongside. We will meet again in Chapter 10.

Chapter 2

Redesigning marketing to fit a different marketplace

don e. schultz

Aims and introduction

Marketing has always been about hopes and dreams. The hope on the part of the marketing organization is that there is, or might be, some 'magic bullet' in the form of a new product or service or a new strategy or a new distribution system that would radically change the world; something that would please customers and, more importantly, make the marketer rich.

Marketers have always been dreamers, too. Much marketing has historically been based on how the marketer believed customers acted and reacted in the marketplace, and how and why they bought what they bought, and why they acted as they did. Much of this was not based on fact but on beliefs and intuition and even the ever-popular 'gut feel' of successful marketers. Self-made merchants did not have to know anything for they operated on instinct, as did inventors and even innovators. The marketing people were often the worst of the lot. All that was needed was a great breakthrough 'creative idea' and sales and profits were assumed to follow.

Yet this sort of 'seat-of-the-pants' marketing worked and it worked well, particularly in the 50 years or so following the Second World War. The world, emerging from a global depression and several years of war on almost every continent except North America and Australia, was eager and anxious to return to the more hedonistic pleasures of housing, refrigerators, cars and even the wonderful new world of detergents and toothpaste and long-lasting deodorants. The world was ripe and ready for traditional marketing, and that is what consumers got: traditional marketing in all its glory and gaudiness, with lots of flashy packages, nifty, new products, massive amounts of mass market advertising and, interestingly, consistently declining prices. Who would not buy into a system like that?

It was during that time period (i.e., the late 1940s and 1950s) that most of the marketing concepts we use today were invented, including share of market distribution formats, retail penetration, mass media advertising, demographics and segmentation. All were either conceived or codified during that time frame, over 50 years ago. And, for the most part, we have not changed those ideas and concepts very much. True, we have enhanced and expanded them, but we have not changed them. Marketers still preach and practise the 4 Ps McCarthy first published in 1960. We still use communication theory developed in the 1930s and 1940s. We still cling to well-worn segmentation schemes based on demographics, geography, sex and income. We still use the 'war-time' analogies such as 'target markets', 'marketing blitzes', 'capturing the initiative' and so on. And, unfortunately, many marketers and much of marketing still operate as they did nearly a half-century ago. For what is supposed to be an innovative science, marketing really has not been very innovative. Enhancements and refinements of existing theory and practice have been the rule of the day.

True, we have added some new concepts and some new approaches over the years: television for one, at least to the extent that, in most consumer marketing plans, everything starts with the television schedule as if it were the be all and end all for marketing communication. We have added more sophisticated statistical approaches, but most are still based on the idea that there is a general mass market with common denominators that can be identified and selected using normal curve distributions. And, although there have been major changes in distribution and retailing, particularly in the form of consolidation and concentration of retail organizations, many marketers still believe in 'channel captains' and 'brand managers', and even the power of 'feet-on-the-street' sales forces. A constant maxim is the more, the better.

So, things really have not changed much in marketing in the last 50 years, at least not in the way the discipline is practised. Even when new external fillips such as the World Wide Web and the Internet have developed, marketers simply tried to adopt and adapt them. But the dot.coms proved that traditional marketing, in spite of the vast amount of money thrown into it, could not make them successful. They were indeed different. True, we have expanded our communication systems to national and global coverage. We have linked markets and marketers and consumers with credit cards and global financial systems. We have added cell phones and SMS (short messaging service). But, in truth, with minor exceptions, marketing is pretty much the way it was when 'I Love Lucy' was in its first run and films were still in black and white.

However, the marketplace has changed and changed substantially. I will not delve into all those changes in much detail in this chapter other than to mention them in passing (they are probably documented in great detail elsewhere in this text). What I will do is focus on the results of those changes and the major impact these activities and alterations have had on how marketing should be practised. Note here that my statement is 'how marketing should be practised', not how it *is* practised, for, there is substantial evidence that the marketplace has changed such that the way we have historically practised the craft must be re-thought and re-worked if it is still to be a relevant concept for the next few decades of the 21st century.

What changed and with what impact?

What changed and how did it impact marketing? The biggest change was technology and the transfer of information. Cairncross (1997) has called it the third transportation revolution. The first was water, the second was air and the third has been electronic (i.e., the ability to transport information, knowledge and even materials by the electronic distribution through voice, video and data). She calls the result, 'The Death of Distance'. It is this demise of the control of distance that has dramatically changed how marketing operates today and how it must function in the future.

Why traditional marketing worked?

In addition to the advantage of time and distance, Cairncross noted traditional marketing worked because the seller commonly knew more than the buyer (i.e., the consumer or customer or, in many cases, even the distributor or wholesaler, or even the retailer). This information advantage gave the marketing organization marketplace power, and that marketplace power allowed the marketing organization to dominate the entire system of supply and demand. The marketing model that emerged from this 'manufacturer-led' system, developed in the 1950s, was one which looked like that shown in Figure 2.1.

As shown, the marketer controlled all the resources and most of all, marketplace information and knowledge. The marketing organization, primarily resting in the hands of manufacturers during that time, decided

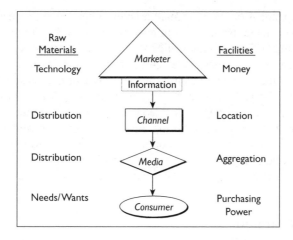

Figure 2.1   Product-driven marketing system

what products to make, when to make them, how many to produce, how to price them, how to distribute them, who they would tell about them, and so on and so on. In other words, the marketer held all the cards, and he or she played them to their best advantage.

The common marketing approach was to:

■ develop several levels of product quality differentiated by price
■ develop limited or extensive distribution as determined by the marketer's goals
■ distribute extensive advertising and promotion to encourage immediate or delayed purchasing
■ manufacture for inventory to generate 'economies of scale'
■ coupon to generate immediate response.

All the tools of marketing were developed during this time, and every one of them assumed an all-powerful marketing organization and a passive or at least responsive distribution system and consumer or end-user that could be managed and manipulated.

The reason the system worked was that the marketer had all the market information and also had control of the technology systems. The retailer had less information (or, at least, fewer resources or facilities to manage the information they did have). The consumer or end-user was totally dependent on the information and/or knowledge the marketer or the channel made available to him or her, commonly through various forms of marketing communication. So, except for the personal experience which the consumer gained from product usage over time or what little they could learn from their immediate circle of friends and the community, they were totally dependent on the marketplace knowledge the marketer and channel system decided to share. No wonder the marketing systems worked. If you had all the information and knowledge and the customer had none, you could dominate the entire territory, and that is just what traditional marketing was all about: control and domination. Moreover, it is what typifies traditional marketing even to this day.

What changed?

In the middle 1970s, the marketplace began to change. Technology, in the form of computers and point-of-sale systems that allowed retailers and distributors and other channel members to capture, store and manage information they normally gathered during the course of their transactions with customers, consumers and end-users became available and most importantly, they became economical to install and use. The technologies, originally designed for inventory control, quickly became converted to end-user data and the power shift was on. Other members of the channel system soon joined in the game (i.e., wholesalers and distributors and agents became skilled in using the new technologies). Most important, the use of those technologies became increasingly economical so rapid development of the systems soon followed. As a result, technology allowed the retailer and the channels to draw down some of the traditional marketplace power held by the manufacturer. That shift is illustrated in Figure 2.2.

As shown, the channel's use of technology gave them more current and useful knowledge about the marketplace than had the manufacturers, who were further upstream. Typically, that knowledge included what consumers were buying, what prices they were willing to pay, when and in what quantity they purchased and so on. As the channels began to consolidate, creating larger, more efficient stores and retailing systems, this information became more valuable and made the channels even more powerful. That is the history of today's retail giants such as Wal-Mart, Carrefours, Home Depot and others. Today, the battle between the manufacturer and the channel has reached a fever pitch with each struggling to hold on to (or increase) the power they have in the

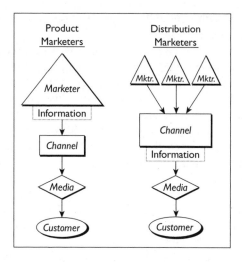

Figure 2.2 Product and distribution marketer charts

marketplace. All, however, are continuing to use traditional marketing systems, and all seem intent on trying to increase their own power within the system.

The big problem is that the marketplace has changed and the marketing struggle they are waging may not even be relevant in the coming decades. The 1970s to early 1990s were the primary time periods during which this diffusion of power from the manufacturer to the distribution channel occurred. That was particularly true in the Western economies. *And then the entire world changed!*

Shifting the power to the consumer or end-user

Much has been written about the Internet, the World Wide Web and the changes those electronic systems have already had and will continue to have in marketing and communication in the years ahead. Just how the development of these electronic interchange, marketing and distribution systems will play out is still the subject of some debate. The failure of the initial dot.com efforts in the marketing arena are well known and well documented. But, those initial failures do not mean that various forms of electronic commerce will not develop in the coming years. We do know the rise of various forms of knowledge and information distribution have already had, and will continue to have, a major impact on the power structure of the marketplace.

During the 1990s, the consumer and end-user began to gain greater information and knowledge about the marketplace, too. Some of that came from the channels and the retailers. As channels and distribution systems expanded, retailers, as a competitive weapon, began to make more knowledge and information available to their customers, the end-users, and thus market knowledge began to diffuse. Granted, the market knowledge the consumers had was still limited to what the manufacturer or retailer chose to share, distribute or provide, but, it was generally much more than the customer had or had access to in the past.

As technology, in the form of interactive, networked information and communication systems, developed following the commercialization of the Internet in the mid-1990s, a slow but inevitable shift of marketplace power occurred which is illustrated in Figure 2.3.

What is most evident from this chart is the dramatic change in the flow of product and service information and market knowledge. As shown in the historic models, those of the product-driven marketer and the distribution-driven channel, the systems were all outbound: that is, products, services, information, knowledge flows and so forth emanated from the manufacturer and channel and flowed out to the customer or consumer through the various media systems to be received and processed by the customers or end-users. Note the inherent assumption that marketers or channels are in control. And that is what almost all

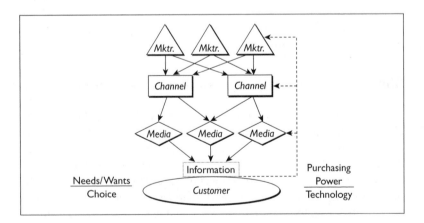

Figure 2.3 Customer-driven marketing system

marketing thought and concepts have been based on: marketers in control, with customers or end-users as receivers or passive recipients of marketer-generated activities.

The new consumer or customer-driven system is different, however, as illustrated above. Because of the diffusion of information technology, the consumer or customer has now been able to take marketplace power from both the manufacturer and channel. And, because information is power, the consumer or customer is rapidly gaining control of the marketplace in every developed economy.

The model is clear. As consumers have more access to information about products, services, prices, quality, location availability and so on, marketplace power shifts inevitably to them. Since they hold the ultimate power (i.e., the ability to purchase or not purchase in order to create or not create income flows for the manufacturer and channels), consumers gain more and more control over the entire marketplace. That power is being taken from the manufacturer and the channel members. Today, the consumer is no longer dependent on what the manufacturer is willing to share or what the channel is willing to make available; the consumer/end-user has gained (or at least has access to) almost perfect marketplace knowledge. And with that knowledge comes power: the power to compare, the power to choose, the power to negotiate, the power to shop throughout the entire world if necessary to find the best available value proposition.

The inevitable shift of technology

Granted, we have only seen the tip of this marketplace power revolution, but the direction is clear and the result inevitable. Marketplace power is shifting through the channel and will ultimately end up in the hands of the consumer and end-user. And that is why traditional marketing, or marketing as it was invented in the 1940s and 1950s, must change, or must at least be adapted to meet the new requirements of a different system with different levels of marketplace power for the various players.

It is true that some forms of traditional marketing will continue to survive and, in some cases, may even continue to prosper. For example, in pharmaceuticals and in some types of high technology, product and channel differentiation may still be possible. Moreover, in some emerging markets such as India, China and Africa, where retail systems provide broader access to products and services for greater groups of the population, power may continue to be held by the channel systems and,

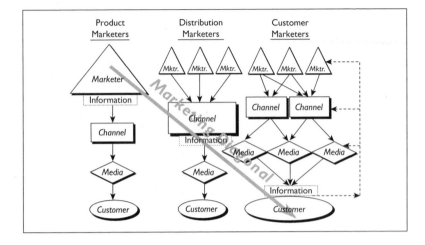

Figure 2.4 The marketing diagonal

in areas where information technology has yet to reach high penetration levels, the old established systems may still prevail; but, for the rest of the established marketing world, traditional 1950s marketing is either dead or dying. It is being replaced as the shift of information technology inevitably slides down the Marketing Diagonal to the customer or end-user. That concept is illustrated in Figure 2.4.

As shown, the shift of information technology generates a shift of marketplace power. Uniquely, each market, each marketer and each system, as shown in the diagram, is different. That is why traditional marketing (i.e., marketing based on generalities, assumptions, averages and so on) will be so difficult to maintain. Generalities do not work any longer, and that is what marketing is based on: generalities, such as assumptions that markets and people and systems are the same, and, most of all, the assumption that the marketer or the channel is in control of the system or can manage the system. It is this realization that provides the context for the major changes that must be made in the marketing systems going forward.

Dealing with the marketplace power shift

Given the scenario described above, what is the future of marketing? Indeed, is there a future for marketing as we know it? And, if so, how can traditional marketing organizations successfully make the transition to this new, customer-driven marketplace? That is important, particularly since it appears that most of the traditional marketing concepts and tools either cannot, will not or do not work and must be changed or adapted to one where some type of 'new marketing' will be possible.

Marketing organizations must make three major structural changes to meet the challenges of the marketplace power shift. The balance of this chapter describes and illustrates those changes. They are described in no particular order although the third (developing financially-based, forward-looking marketing approaches) will probably take the longest to implement and will require the greatest structural change; but it will also provide the greatest returns to the marketing firm.

Multiple marketing models and structures

Inherent in the three marketplace structures we have described above is the requirement that marketing organizations of the future have multiple marketing systems or marketing structures in place and operating, not just a single system which has been the tradition since marketing began. This idea of multiple marketing systems flies in the face of traditional marketing organizational wisdom, research and practice. Historically, marketers have sought to find the single best marketplace approach and then apply that approach to all their operations. Indeed, most of the marketing strategy approaches that have been developed assume the selection of a 'best for the marketing organization' format.

For example, Porter's (1985) strategic model, which has been updated and expanded since then, suggests that marketers select one marketing strategy and hew to it continuously for success. Or, if the selected strategy is to be changed, it must be done with care and consideration. Marketers can select from 'price', 'differentiation', or 'focus' as alternate strategies. While these may overlap to some degree, Porter's recommendation is that there must be one single, clear-cut, and identifiable go-to-market strategy. Marketers and marketing have bought into this concept. Thus, the traditional marketing management approach has been to develop a marketing planning, development and execution model that fits the organization, not necessarily the customer. Again, we see an illustration of an assumed-to-be-dominant marketer who is in control of the marketplace.

Indeed, we have used the same approach in developing the three marketer scenarios shown in Figures 2.1–4 above. We have illustrated single systems for each marketplace and assumed the marketer could, would, should or is indeed implementing only one of those systems. Figure 2.4 on p. 20 serves as a reminder of those three marketplaces and the Marketing Diagonal that illustrates the shift of marketplace power as a result of the shift of marketplace power (see Schultz and Kitchen, 2000).

In the way we have used the model above, we have taken the marketer's viewpoint: that is, how the marketer or marketing organization would approach the marketplace. The inherent assumption, however, is that there are customers and prospects who would like to operate in, or prefer operating in, one of the three models. For example, there are doubtless customers who are or will be totally happy with the product marketing model: that is, they are quite content to have the marketer control the system (i.e., decide what products to manufacture and bring to market), determine the general pricing levels, identify and make available advertising and promotion advising and informing them about what is being offered, and so on. In short, these customers and consumers like and are comfortable with the existing, traditional marketing system and see little or no reason for it to change or for them to ask for any change.

Other customers prefer the distribution or channel-driven model where the retailer or channel partner evaluates the marketplace for product and service alternatives. The channel then stocks them in a store or other distribution facility. The customer then selects from the assortment the channel has assembled. This is the traditional retailing system with which 20th-century customers are so familiar. It appears to be one that will continue for some time to come.

Increasingly, though, we are seeing some groups of customers and prospects who prefer to make most of the marketplace decisions for themselves. They enjoy the search for new or different products, want to make comparisons, and enjoy the convenience and speed of on-line or Web-based shopping through the Internet. Or it may simply be that these customers want more control over the choices and decisions they make regarding products and services they purchase or use and enjoy.

The problem for the marketer is that there are at least these three marketing systems or approaches presently in place. Most likely, given the opportunity, customers and prospects may well identify or find they prefer other alternatives or choices on how to deal with the various marketing organizations. Obviously, this places the traditional marketing concept of having one system, one approach and one strategy in great jeopardy. It raises the question for the marketer: 'If I don't have a marketing system that reflects how customers want to buy, will they be likely to go to other vendors or suppliers?' The answer to that question, at least at the opening of the 21st century, is undoubtedly a resounding '*Yes*'.

So, what is a marketer to do?

On the one hand, there is the traditional intellectual argument, not to mention the bottom-line efficiency, of having a single marketing system. The approach seems to make eminent good sense to the marketer and from that standpoint will be the most effective use of finite corporate resources. On the other hand, there is the increasing power of the customer and consumer which demands marketing systems to fit their own needs, not just those of the marketing organization. If the marketer adheres to a single system, some customers are, at some point, bound to fall away. If the marketer implements multiple approaches or multiple marketing systems, the management, operation and control over those multiple systems become an enormous task.

In our view, the answer then is that there must be a total restructuring of the marketing organization, so that marketing organizations are built around customers, not around distribution systems. By taking this approach, the marketing firm begins to focus on the elements and activities that are important to customers, not just to the marketing organization. It begins to relate the firm's marketing efforts to marketing returns and

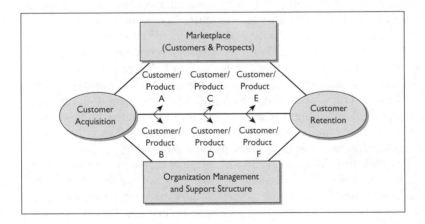

Figure 2.5 Customer management structure

outcomes, not just outputs. It encourages the marketing organization to focus its efforts and resources on how it should invest its time and effort in going forwards. Thus, it looks forward to generating potential future returns, not just maintaining a system that has worked in the past.

Figure 2.5 illustrates a conceptual model of how a marketing organization might be structured in the future. It takes into consideration the four major areas of customer marketing (i.e., acquiring, retaining, growing or migrating customers through a product portfolio). Further, it fits well with the 21st-century financial requirements of how a marketing firm invests its resources and measures the resulting returns.

As shown above, most marketing organizations are focused on four types of investments, including marketing investments, as shown below.

- To acquire new customers
- To retain present customers
- To grow the value of present customers
- To migrate customers through the product or service portfolio (i.e., to replacement-sell, up-sell, cross-sell, and so on).

As shown, the marketing organization is designed to achieve certain goals with customers. The acquisition team focuses on acquiring new customers. They determine how, where and in what manner customers would like to do business with the firm. If the customer or prospect has sufficient value, a distribution or marketing system can or would be developed or employed which would fit that customer's needs.

The retention team focuses on continuity of customer purchase and maintenance of income flows. Thus, this group studies and understands why customers do business with the firm today and how they might want to do business with the firm in the future. Their primary attention is focused on why customers might defect or churn out of the customer base. If the customer value is sufficient, the retention team would be charged with finding a way to satisfy the customer and keep them as part of the firm's income base both now and in the future.

Inside this customer-oriented organization are teams of marketers who are responsible for understanding customers well enough to be able to identify the potential future use present customers might have for existing products or services (i.e., the now-famous 'increase the share-of-wallet or share-of-requirements' concept). That simply means growing the sales and profits of existing customers. This team would also be responsible for what we have termed 'customer migration': that is, identifying other products or services the organization might currently have or might acquire that would better fill the needs and wants of existing customers. This might include encouraging customers to trade up to, or cross over to, another product or service in the marketer's line that might provide a better value for the customer or a better return for the organization.

It is clear from this approach that the organization is designed to fill customer needs and wants by providing the type of marketing organization and structure the customer desires, not just implementing the type of marketing that it is easiest or most economical for the marketing organization to employ. It takes away the monolithic formats of how the 'firm goes to market'. It substitutes instead an approach that suggests the organization is ready and willing to serve customers in the form and fashion they prefer.

This approach also challenges many marketers' pre-conceived notions of how customers should, could or might do business with the firm. Most of all, this new marketing structure helps the company serve a broad array of customers and prospects, not just those who will accept the method and manner in which the marketing organization has always operated.

With this view of multiple marketing systems, we can now look at the marketing and communication activities of firms operating in the three marketplace systems and how those can and must be changed to succeed in the 21st century.

Reversing the flow of marketing efforts

Traditionally, as illustrated in the first two marketing models in the Marketing Diagonal, marketing systems and approaches have been designed for an outbound flow: that is, the processes assume the marketer or marketing organization has control of the marketplace, which means the company determines how the firm would like to deliver products and services, communication, customer service and all the other traditional marketing factors and functions (see Figure 2.4 on p. 20).

The product-marketer and distribution-marketer systems assume the marketer is in control of the marketing process. Thus, he or she holds the power to determine the marketing approaches, marketing communication, the pricing and so on. The marketer, having made all those decisions, then sends those marketing activities and actions out through various forms of media or other distribution channels to reach the preselected audiences they believe would be most responsive.

Thus, today, most marketing systems are based on outbound flows (i.e., the marketer moving their programmes and activities out towards customers or prospects). While this approach gives the marketer great control over the process, it tends to be very costly and generally inefficient to operate. The marketer is continuously sending marketing programmes, messages, offers, advertising and so on out into the marketplace in an attempt to gain some type of marketplace response. As a result, the marketing costs are always up-front for the marketer. While the argument is made that those marketing costs are re-captured in the price received from the customer who chooses to purchase, the system, in and of itself, is terribly inefficient and produces great waste not just for the marketing firm, but for the customer and society as well.

When we contrast the first two models with the new customer–marketer model, the difference becomes immediately clear. The new 21st-century customer–marketer model is networked and interactive. Thus, with control in the hands of the customer or consumer, the distribution of marketing activities becomes one which is driven by the user of the system, not the owner of the system. Customers access and acquire products, services, information, comparisons, knowledge and so on when they need it or when they would like to have it, not when the marketer decides to make it available. Thus our new customer–marketer system is, for the most part, inbound, not outbound.

This change raises some interesting questions since it directly challenges the traditional marketing communication systems that are in place (i.e., things such as advertising, sales promotion, direct marketing, public relations, events and the plethora of other marketing and communication activities that have been developed over the years: see Kitchen and Schultz, 2001).

Changing the theory

In an outbound marketing system, the marketer primarily relies on traditional communication theory: that is, there is a sender (in this case, the marketer); there is a message or what the marketer wants to say or transmit to the customer or prospect; there is also some form of media (i.e., newspapers, the postal service, television, radio, etc.), and, finally, there is the receiver. In a marketing system, that commonly means a customer or consumer or prospect. Those are the people to whom almost all the marketing and marketing communication programmes are directed. A simple illustration of this historical marketing communication system is shown as Figure 2.6.

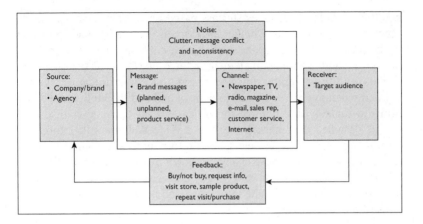

Figure 2.6 Interactive marketing communication model

Source: Tom Duncan, *IMC: Using Advertising and Promotion to Build Brands* (2001), published by Irwin/McGraw-Hill. Published with permission.

This model is derived from Duncan and is based on the Schramm and Roberts model (1971). There is a sender, a message, a medium through which the message is delivered and a receiver; but there are also two other factors that influence the communication system. The first is 'noise'. 'Noise' consists of factors that restrict the flow or comprehension of information transfer as the message moves from sender to receiver. That is shown in the top box in the model. As illustrated, 'noise' can consist of media clutter, message conflict, inconsistency in the marketer's messages and so forth. In these cases, the 'noise' comes primarily from external sources, although some may also be internally generated. In any case, 'noise' affects the transmission of the message and the receipt, understanding and acceptance by the customer or receiver.

The other factor in the communication model is called 'feedback'. This so-called 'feedback loop' is how the marketing organization determines whether or not the receiver or customer or prospect saw, heard or responded to the marketing message or activities. Commonly, in a traditional outbound marketing system, the marketer evaluates the 'feedback' by measuring such things as whether or not the customer or prospect bought or did not buy, whether they visited a retail outlet, whether they made a repeat purchase and so on. Clearly, in a marketing sense, the firm in the traditional 'sender–receiver' model is trying to determine whether or not the marketing programme worked.

The customer or consumer, shown as the 'receiver' in the model above, is simply an element in the process. The marketer is in control and the marketer determines success based on whether or not goals or objectives were met, not whether the marketing activities had any value to the receiver. As shown, the customer or consumer has no input into the system and is simply an element in the process.

This traditional marketing and marketing communication system worked when the marketer was in control and had the ability and capability to manage and control the process. That changed radically in the 1990s when the Internet, the World Wide Web and other forms of customer-controlled, often electronic, information and communication technology emerged. These changes, shown by the Marketing Diagonal in our previous discussion, have totally changed the way marketing systems work. We call these the interactive and networked marketing systems of the 21st century.

Networked and interactive marketing systems

When customers were given access to technology and became able to access marketing information at their leisure, the marketplace changed and changed radically. No longer were they dependent on the marketer or the channel to provide product or service or usage information; suddenly, they could access that information whenever and wherever they needed it. Search engines such as Google, Netscape and Yahoo aggregated and synthesized information and knowledge from all over the world. That generally provided all the information a customer or prospect needed to make intelligent and informed comparative product and service decisions. It is true that not all consumers or customers have access to these systems at this time, and neither do all of those consumers who have access to the systems make full use of their capabilities; but the direction is clear. The customer, not the marketer, will be in control of the 21st-century marketplace. This change of control really defines how, where and in what manner marketers will or must go to market in the future.

In an earlier section, we described the traditional outbound marketing system. In Figure 2.7, we illustrate the interactive and networked system as a comparison. As shown, the customer has control and can buy from any system or through any market unit that appeals to or provides the best value for the customer. While the shift of control is important, perhaps more important is the change which the networked and interactive system implies for the marketer. Instead of being outbound as it traditionally has been, the new marketing systems become inbound. In other words, the customer becomes the sender and the marketing organization becomes the receiver. While there are still messages and media systems

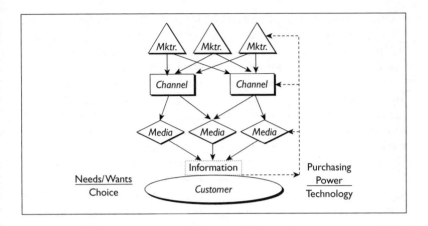

Figure 2.7   Customer marketplace

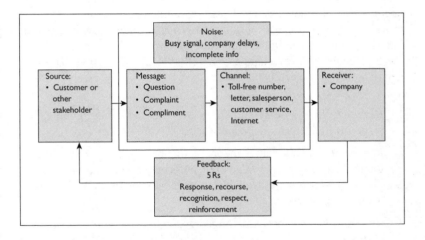

Figure 2.8   Customer-initiated communication model

Source: Tom Duncan. Published with permission.

involved, they are totally different, as shown. It is this reversal of roles that 21st-century marketers must understand.

We identify the new 'sender' on the left-hand side of the model as the customer or other stakeholder in Figure 2.8. The 'message', instead of being a persuasive message sent by the marketer, becomes an question, a complaint, a compliment or other message from the customer directed towards the marketer.

The channel changes dramatically as it is no longer a mass or even a targeted medium approach. It is, instead, a direct channel from the customer to the marketing organization (i.e., a toll-free telephone number, a letter sent by the customer, a contact or request from a sales person, contact with the customer service centre or even an inquiry through the Web or Internet). Just as clearly, the receiver of the message becomes the company or the marketing organization. Indeed, we have totally reversed the flow of information and material in this model and put the marketing organization in a completely different situation.

The 'noise' in the system changes as well. Now, the noise is created by the marketing organization rather than by external factors. Because the customer is inquiring or contacting the marketing firm, the lack of communication occurs because the marketer does not have sufficient telephone lines to handle incoming calls, is unable to respond to customer or prospect requests, sends incomplete information in response to a customer request, fails to answer the customer's inquiry properly or for a host of other reasons. Thus, the marketing and communication process fails not because of some external problem, but, because of internal problems within the marketing organization.

The 'feedback loop' changes as well. 'Feedback' is now based on what Duncan (2001) calls the 5 Rs:

1 *Response*: how quickly and completely the marketing organization responds to the customer or prospect.

2 *Recourse*: what alternative the marketing organization offers the customer if the answers provided or the information sent was insufficient. What alternatives are available to the customer to find solutions to his or her inquiry?

3 *Recognition*: did the marketing organization recognize a valuable customer or welcome a new prospect? Did the customer feel the response was genuine or was the response cursory and generalized?

4 *Respect*: was the customer treated with respect (or at least with what the customer thought was respect) so that he or she wants to begin or continue doing business with the marketing firm?

5 *Reinforcement*: did the activities in the 'feedback loop' reinforce the image, value, relationship between the customer and the marketer, or did it initiate a beginning of those feelings and situations with the prospect?

From this perspective the new, inbound marketing system requires many changes on many fronts by marketing organizations. But the question remains: why would or should the marketing organization encourage this new 'reversed-role' approach? The answer is simple: *money*!

The system, as outlined above is much more efficient for all parties. Waste in the form of unused or unwanted advertising messages, direct mail shots, events or even sponsorships is reduced. Thus, the system becomes much more practical and useful. From the viewpoint of the customer, information, material, knowledge, and so on are available when and where and in what form he or she wants or needs (i.e., marketing information on a 24–7 basis and at a cost he or she appears to be willing to pay).

The problem, of course, is that this approach challenges almost all the present marketing systems. Media systems are designed to carry outbound messages and incentives: those are challenged. Traditional outbound marketing distribution is questioned as to whether or not customers want to buy in that fashion or whether it is simply the way the marketing organization wants to sell. Many of the functional specialists who have grown up in the traditional outbound marketing systems are challenged as the shift from outbound to inbound occurs.

Most of all, the stewardship of traditional marketing and communication comes under attack. In the outbound systems, much of the measurement of marketing and communication is based on the counting or estimating of the volume of messages sent out. In this inbound system, accountability becomes very clear and concise. Either the customer or the prospect contacted the marketer, or he or she did not. Thus, measurement of returns on marketing and communication become simply a matter of counting the inquiries, questions or even sales. And customer satisfaction measures change as well: these become clearer when the number or questions or concerns from customers either rises or falls based on the marketing and communication efforts.

While this system appears to have great value, there will probably be great resistance, particularly from the media organizations which are accustomed to carrying the outbound messages. Functional specialists such as direct marketers, advertising executives, public relations people and so on will resist the concept simply because it makes their skills and capabilities less valuable; but the change will come and for one simple reason: it makes economic good sense for both the marketer and the buyer. We deal with that third and final issue next.

Developing forward-looking financial measurement methodologies

Marketing has been trapped by psychology. Having no solid theory base, marketing and marketing communication people have adopted or adapted concepts from other fields to try to explain what has been called the 'marketing system'. In its most basic form, marketing attempts to illustrate or describe and develop relevant approaches to deal with the actions and interactions between a group of buyers and sellers. Thus, marketers can illustrate and explain the 'hard-wired' concepts of the marketplace (i.e., manufacturing, new product development, pricing, distribution channels and so on). That is what is illustrated in a very simplified way in the three marketplace marketing systems described previously.

While the models are simple, they are an attempt to illustrate the actions and activities of the various players involved. Thus, the models illustrate the flow of the various buying and selling activities that occur in the marketplace and how they are related.

Why marketing has trouble explaining financial value

To provide an explanation of how the various 'marketing systems' work, marketers and marketing academics have built models. Marketing, because it is based on the concept that 'organizations are developed to serve customers', has thus generally focused on the customer or end-user as the basis for the models. Since, for the most part, end-users are people or firms (here we focus on consumer marketing since that is the basis of most marketing theory), marketers have adapted or adopted basic psychological models to explain or illustrate much marketing thought. Thus, marketers have attempted to explain how marketing systems work by using some type of psychological model, often under the terminology of consumer or organizational behaviour, or communication theory such as was described in the previous section. They have tried to explain how and why buyers buy, how and why sellers sell, how and why channel members act and re-act as they do, how advertising and marketing communication communicate, how customers and prospects respond, and so on.

The problem is that marketing, in a business sense, is not a psychological model at all; it is a financial model. The organization sets up marketing departments not to learn how customers buy or how they should sell, but to improve the returns on their product or service investments.

The system is: £x into marketing and marketing activities with the expectation that those investments will generate financial returns now or sometime in the future. For every £x spent on marketing there will ideally be > £x back to the firm as a result of those investments. Psychology is nice and it gives the managers in the organization warm, fuzzy feelings to think they understand their customers and their needs and wants. But, at the end of the day (at least from a senior management viewpoint), marketing is, or should be, all £x with some other sense perhaps thrown in.

We would thus argue that marketing managers have fallen into the psychology trap: that is, they have built many of their explanatory models using attitudinal measures. The stem cell of all attitudinal and psychological marketing methodology seems to have come from the so-called 'Hierarchy of Effects' advertising model developed by Lavidge and Steiner (1960). That was closely followed by a similar concept developed by Colley (1961) and promulgated by the Association of National Advertisers in the United States at about the same time. A stylized version of the Lavidge and Steiner model is shown in Figure 2.9.

As shown, consumers are assumed to move through a series of attitudinal-change steps on the way to making a purchase decision. Those steps are clearly identified and, supposedly, the consumer's progress through the system can be tracked and charted. The hierarchy is an intuitively appealing system that seems to have a fairly clear and consistent beginning, middle and end: in short, a great marketing story. Note particularly in the model that the marketer has total control of the system or process. By implementing various forms of marketing and communication activities, the customer can be pulled or pushed or

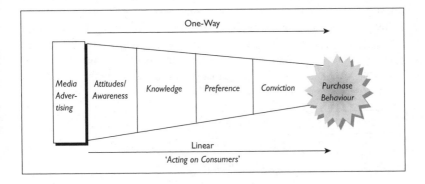

Figure 2.9   Traditional 'advertising-based' view of communications

manipulated or managed through the process. The model is clearly one of 'marketer in control, customer as respondent'.

In the diffusing marketplaces we described in the Marketing Diagonal model, it is clear that while this psychological model may have been very relevant in the 1960s, it likely can and should be challenged on a number of fronts today, yet this 'Hierarchy of Effects' model still provides the base for most marketing planning and certainly all media buying and evaluation by even the most sophisticated marketing organizations around the world.

While one could argue that the 'Hierarchy of Effects' model is useful in terms of developing marketing and communication plans that might perhaps ultimately influence future customers and prospects, it has little to do with how marketing and communication influences existing customers who are already buying. And, for most organizations, those are the key players in their marketing systems.

Further, this model leaves much to be desired from an economic standpoint. The problem, of course, is that it has proved almost impossible to connect the psychological elements of attitudinal changes to any type of financial model of consumer or customer behaviour. In short, people do not respond the way they are supposed to, and neither do they always do what they say. Thus, knowing that attitudes have changed has little to do with building an economic model of marketing investment and return. The difficulty of identifying how much advertising or communication or marketing is needed to move the customer or prospect through the system or process has proved to be a Gordian knot for the marketing profession.

The basic economic question is quite simple: the marketer invests finite resources, generally in the form of the marketing budget, to purchase marketing activities that are supposed to influence customer behaviour, but the measurement systems do not provide financial returns; they provide attitudinal returns that commonly have little or no financial value. So, the questions senior management continues to ask and which marketers, even at the most senior level, are unable to answer, are as follows:

- How much should we invest in marketing?
- What will we get back in terms of financial returns?
- Over what time period will those returns occur?

Clearly, these are all financial or economic questions and they demand some type of financial or economic model for answers. But, until recently, marketing has not been able to provide anything more than attitudinal measurement responses.

Changing the measurement system

With the advent of technology (i.e., the ability of the marketing organization to capture, store, manage and manipulate behavioural information about what customers or end-users actually did or have done in the marketplace), the development of economic marketing models has rapidly increased. For example, the current state-of-the-art forms of measurement now include an approach called 'Marketing Mix Modelling (MMM)'. This has done much to explain the financial impact, effects and returns from various historical marketing and communication activities and initiatives.

MMM (see www.pdi.com and www.mma.com) was used initially to help explain the historical returns on various forms of marketing communication for consumer product marketers (i.e., fast moving consumer goods, or fmcg). Using a variation of statistical regression analysis, MMM is now being expanded into other areas of marketing activities and it appears to hold much promise for the future.

In its simplest form, MMM uses historical sales results as the base for the analysis. Various marketing and promotional programmes that appeared during that same time-frame are then statistically compared to determine their influence and impact and their value in generating incremental returns. These incremental returns provide an indication of what sales value was obtained from the financial investment in the various marketing activities. An illustration of the type of analysis that Marketing Mix Modelling provides is illustrated in Figures 2.10–12.

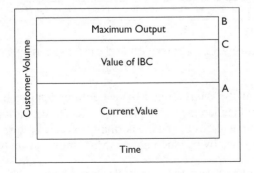

Figure 2.10   Marketing mix model

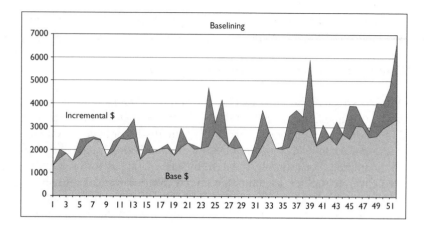

Figure 2.11   Parsing out incremental returns

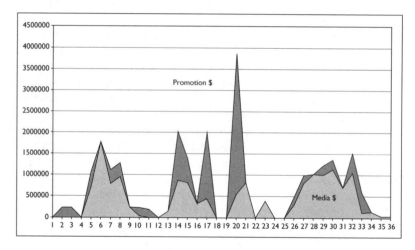

Figure 2.12   Promotion and media spending in the
Los Angeles market

As shown, the Marketing Mix Modelling approach statistically
separates out the incremental impact and effect of the various marketing
activities from what would be the normally expected returns by the marketing firm. Thus, by conducting an MMM study, the analyst can say:

Based on historical data, here is the level of business we would have expected to
do in this period. However, because of what we invested in various marketing and

communication activities, this is the actual level of business that was done. We can attribute these incremental returns to these marketing activities.

Therefore, by comparing the incremental returns achieved compared to the costs of the marketing programmes employed, estimates or calculations of return on investment (ROI) can be developed.

In Figure 2.11, this is shown as 'incremental returns' as a result of the various marketing and communication investments which the organization made. In Figure 2.12, further analysis has been conducted to illustrate what made up that incremental increase. In this case, it was composed of returns from advertising and promotion investments in the markets analysed.

Through this type of economic analysis, marketers are beginning to parse out the financial or economic returns from their previous marketing investments. But unfortunately this type of analysis, while useful is still basically 'looking over the shoulder' accounting. In other words, it helps explain what happened but it does little to help predict what might occur in the future. To be a valuable analytical tool, marketing must be able to estimate or predict what might occur in the future. In other words, marketing needs some methodology to estimate or calculate how various activities might create value going forward, and not just report on estimated results from the past. Fortunately, some new methodologies are being developed that might be able to provide the answers. We will look at these next.

Building future value with marketing

Marketers have always been interested in the future, and what might, could or should happen next. Unfortunately, having bought into the psychological models such as the Hierarchy of Effects, they have had little success in the prediction business. Fortunately, it does appear that financial models hold much more promise, and that is what we focus on in this section.

To build financial or economic models of marketing investment and return, the first requirement is to walk away from the historical psychological models. That means treating marketing and marketing investments as financial models, pure and simple (i.e., determining what and where the future source of income will be to the marketing organization), and that means customers. It is, in truth, that simple. Customers create the income flows for organizations now and into the future. Few other organizational activities make any contribution to the income of the organization. It is customers that count. Therefore, it is customers' actions that must be counted. So the first step in building a marketing financial model is (a) to identify the firm's customers and (b) to identify the flow of income they create for the organization over time. (Note: in the discussion below, we have taken a very broad overview of the process used to identify and value customers and their income flows: see Schultz and Walters, 1997, and Schultz and Kitchen, 2000, for a more detailed description of the process.)

First, the marketer must understand that various customers create differing levels of costs and returns. We start with the idea that customers are the assets of the firm and must be managed in that way. Figure 2.13 shows this in diagrammatic form.

We must determine the value of a customer based on his or her current level of purchases from the organization at the contribution margin line. This identifies the net value of the customer or group of customers to the firm. Of equal importance is the potential value that customer might have in the future. Thus, the calculation to be made is the current value of the customer plus an estimate of the total value the customer creates for all other organizations selling in the same category.

This estimation is called the 'share of wallet', 'share of garage', 'share of stomach', to name but a few. In essence, it tells the marketing organization the current value of the customer or customer group and what the potential value of the customer or customer group might be in

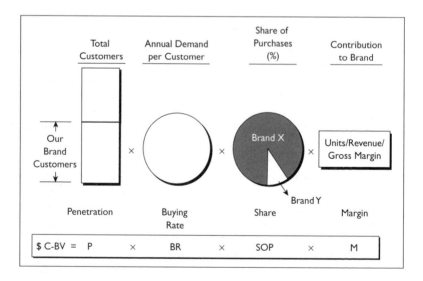

Figure 2.13   What customers are worth

the future, and identifies a likely upper limit. It is this future value that will be important, as we will see in a few moments.

By knowing a customer's current and potential value, the marketer can then move to a 'closed-loop' approach to marketing. In other words, how much value is currently in place? How much potential is available? Therefore, how much would the marketer be willing to invest to (i) acquire a totally new customer, (ii) retain a current customer at the present return level, (iii) grow the present customer by increasing the marketer's share of value or requirements (or whatever), or (iv) invest to migrate the customer through the organization's product or service portfolio? That concept is illustrated in Figure 2.14.

Once the customer's value is known, a decision can be made on what level of investment might be made. Then measurements or changes in customer value can be determined. Thus, the marketer will have created a 'closed-loop' financial marketing model. Since the model is 'closed-loop', the marketer can measure and learn from the various marketing activities over time. This 'test and learn' methodology is and will be the heart of 'future value' marketing in the 21st century. Knowing the value of the customer, understanding the financial impact of various marketing and communication activities and being able to then estimate or calculate returns on investments, marketers will move from 'hopes and dreams' to facts and financial values. It is here, in the development of financial measures, that the future of marketing will lie rather than in the

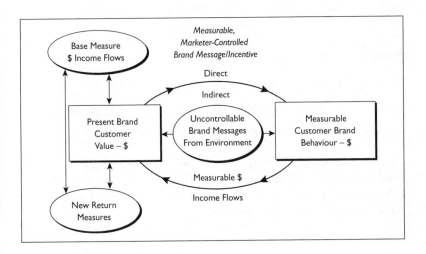

Figure 2.14   Closed-loop systems

traditional attitudinal measures that have been developed over the years. While attitudes and psychological measures are useful, they will be used to explain consumer behaviour, not to predict consumer behaviour in the future. This may well be the most important marketing change of all.

With this view of the need for financial measures of marketing and communication, we have completed our discussion of marketing in the 21st century.

Some final thoughts

In this chapter, we have tried to paint a picture of what marketing is, what marketing has been, and what marketing should be in the 21st century. There is much value in marketing theory, as there is much value in how marketing has developed over the past half-century. There is also much value to the models and approaches that have been created, but the marketplace has changed and marketing must change as well.

There will probably always be areas and customers and marketing organizations that can operate successfully in the traditional product-marketer mode. By the same token, it is clear that the marketplace has changed and will doubtless continue to change, and so there is a need to understand and be able to adapt to the demands of a customer–marketer system. It is this ability to adapt and change that is critical to the success of the entire field of marketing as it moves forward. Being grounded in the past is good, but clinging to that past in the face of current change is not. Thus, marketing has to adapt and change.

Although there are many changes that are required, we have suggested to astute marketers just three changes in this chapter:

- the acceptance of multiple marketing systems
- the need to move from outbound to inbound flows of marketing
- the need for financial models of marketing investments and returns.

Doubtless other needs will develop as the 21st century unfolds. But we believe that if these three are widely adopted, marketing will present a new, innovative, and thus a richer and more diverse, field for management and academics in the 21st century.

Rethinking the value concept in marketing

3

w. fred van raaij and theo poiesz

Aims

In this chapter, a new approach to the value concept in marketing is proposed. A number of trends in the marketing environment are forcing marketing to rethink its position and future. Consumer needs and wants change and they are seeking new aspects in brands, products, services, and corporate entities. But modern consumers are unable or unwilling to maximize their utility for all aspects of their expenditures. They often prefer pre-selections by retailers and all-in-one solutions to 'problems' such as insurance and finance needs. Thus technology and interactive media will have a growing impact on consumers. And yet, at the same time, proliferation of products and brands and their advertising create information overload with consumers. Product innovations can often easily be imitated by others suppliers. With an unchanged approach, marketing will create its own decline. We propose a future scenario with three aspects:

(a) an integration of products and services into cross-domain packages;

(b) long-term relationships of suppliers and customers; and

(c) information technology to create databases and interaction between suppliers and customers and to create customization of products and services to individual characteristics and desires.

In this chapter, we sketch the contours of a future of marketing to accommodate these trends in the marketing environment.

Paradigm shift?

For any discipline, both academic and professional, it is important periodically to reconsider its paradigm. A paradigm refers to the most generic approach of the discipline. It consists of a number of principles that are generally assumed to be so self-evident that their application is usually implicit (Kuhn, 1970). The principles refer to the general types of theories, concepts, methods and techniques. The paradigm involves the most general way of 'doing things', and may be described as the dominant culture of a discipline. This, in itself, indicates that a paradigm, just like a culture, usually covers a long period of time. During such a period, its implicit rules and principles are taken for granted. New data and evidence are gathered along the same line of thinking. Then, at some stage, results and new developments appear that do not fit the dominant paradigm. This prompts the onset of a different way of thinking, resulting in criticism regarding the dominant approach. Defenders of the dominant paradigm are attacked by others who no longer believe in the current paradigm (Lakatos, 1968). The firm basis for decisions, trade-offs and behaviour starts to crumble. If the attackers 'defeat' the defenders of the old paradigm, they will start developing a new paradigm (van Raaij, 1985). Paradigms can be seen as long cycles in a discipline's history.

Often the reason for the decline of a paradigm can be found in the external context of the discipline. For example, important changes may take place in the environment, which may mean that the current paradigm no longer applies to the new situation, and may need adaptation or even replacement.

The question of whether a paradigm shift is imminent may be asked in anticipation when a discipline is confronted with sudden and dramatic changes in its environment. It may even be necessary to anticipate the change when considerable interests are involved. It is better to construct a future scenario and be prepared than to sit back and wait for it to happen. We feel that dramatic and important changes are now taking place in the context of marketing. Marketing plays an important role in the economies of Western societies, and therefore we consider it necessary to address the question of whether the prevalent marketing paradigm is subject to change within the near future. If this question can be answered in a positive way, the next question is whether this will change the roles and interactions of the parties involved.

But what is 'marketing'?

In order to prepare our answer to the first question, we will take the following approach. First, we will critically analyse the nature of marketing, its current paradigm, the changes in its context, and the possible implications of context changes for the marketing paradigm. If the results provide a reason to continue with our analysis, we will also explore the future relationship between product/service providers and consumers and the nature of the marketing instruments that may be important in this relationship. For a practice-orientated discipline such as marketing it makes no sense to consider a future too far away. The speed of change requires a realistic time-frame. For this reason, we set our future scope at about five years from the present, or towards the end of the first decade of the 21st century, as we feel that this is the period that may be considered without engaging in mere guesswork.

The type of analysis that we will adopt is qualitative in nature, as the future does not provide for a rigorous empirical analysis and therefore we will make use of qualitative extrapolations. On the basis of arguments we want to present a general view on marketing developments and a vision of a future marketing scenario. This is based on a book recently published in Dutch (Poiesz and van Raaij, 2002).

The fundamental discussion we are about to enter requires an assessment of the core meaning of marketing and the identification of its current paradigm. What is marketing? This seemingly simple question is, in fact, quite complex. It may be argued that the identification of the paradigm directly depends on the marketing definition: the two are closely related. An inadequate definition may put us on the wrong foot in the analysis of the paradigm and may mislead us into paying attention to mere aspects of marketing that do not cover its full meaning. Thus, we should be aware of the risk that a definition may only identify what is directly visible such as, for example, marketing management or the use of marketing instruments. Rather than scratching the surface of marketing, we should focus on its essence: what does it stand for? The answer to this question ultimately affects the nature of marketing policy decisions.

This is not the place to give an inventory of all the definitions that have been provided of marketing. There is no single, generally accepted definition; in fact, each individual marketing textbook seems to have its own definition. (By the way, in only very few of these textbooks has the nature of the marketing paradigm been addressed.) In spite of the many definitions of marketing, its core meaning seems to be blurred. In the definition we want to present here, marketing is *the process of creating the experience of surplus value for all parties involved*. Marketing is a value augmentation discipline and is successful if all parties benefit in a win–win situation. The reference to multiple parties prevents the definition from covering exchanges such as charity, theft or one-sided exploitation. This means that we do not want to view marketing as involving the mere production of value. If party A provides party B with a product that party B asks for, this is not necessarily marketing, even if the product or service has a value for party B. Marketing should not be equated with the realization of transactions. Neither do we take marketing as a summary term for the deployment of marketing instruments, for the simple reason that marketing should not be confused with the mere intention to provide value. Although the word 'marketing' is often used to designate the conceptualization, planning, and implementation of marketplace activities, this implies a distraction from its core meaning. Our definition stresses the implementation of the intention, the result of activities. The only thing that counts is that incremental value will be experienced. We argue that this is the core meaning which explains why the role of marketing is of great importance for economic growth. Without the experienced surplus value, the market supply will become homogeneous (commodities), prices will fall, and investments will drop. This reduces market supply variety even more. Therefore, an analysis of whether the core meaning of marketing is vulnerable to contextual changes seems to be warranted.

With the help of the notion of the experienced surplus value, the paradigm may be determined. (By the way, we realize the catch involved in the present type of argumentation: the definition and the paradigm of marketing may artificially support each other, suggesting a higher validity of their interpretation than is justified.) We will assess to what extent the current general approach to marketing is characterized by the elements contained in our definition: the experience of surplus value by all parties involved. In doing so, we will focus on marketing to end-buyers or consumers and will not consider business-to-business marketing, although the latter type of marketing and consumer marketing are strongly related.

Changing consumers

Let us start our analysis by making a contrast between two consumers. Consumer A is an elaborate decision-maker. She experiences a need for a new household appliance that will help her to reduce the time spent on chores. She makes an inventory of the product types and brands in the market. The information that she needs to assess, price and quality, is provided by advertising, in-store information and packages. Additional information is acquired from store personnel, experienced lay persons, and persons in her social environment. She is very able to distinguish the relevant features of the various products and brands, and is equally capable of comparing different purchase options. After a careful trade-off, the consumer makes a choice, pays for the product, and uses it in accordance with the intentions of the producer and the instructions in the manual. In a product satisfaction survey, the consumer indicates satisfaction with the product, and indicates the reasons why. When the product approaches economic, psychological or technical old age (whichever comes first), she replaces it before it breaks down. The experiences with the previous product are taken into account when making trade-offs among different purchase options.

Consumer B has some interest in a household appliance, but he experiences considerable difficulties in assessing its particular functions and quality. The technological sophistication requires considerable expertise for a quality judgement. Evidently, this expertise is not available. Because of his high discretionary income, the consumer decides to buy it anyway, but the choice is not made on the basis of its inherent characteristics. Rather, it is based on the idea that the brand is well-known. This idea, in turn, is based on a subjective interpretation of the frequency by which the brand is advertised in the mass media. After the purchase, he uses the product. However, whether he uses the product to his maximum advantage remains unknown. Some of its features are sometimes used; some other features happen to be forgotten. The manual is never consulted. In a satisfaction survey, the consumer decides to tick the box that stands for 'satisfied' for the mere reason that it seems awkward to do otherwise. After all, he does not have a reason to complain. The open question on the reasons for the provided answer is left unanswered, however. The product is replaced when a new design is introduced in the market. If the product breaks down before that, the consumer cannot judge why, and neither can he determine whether his consumption style played a role. When the appliance is replaced, the choice is based very much on first impressions and associations: 'This design looks so good, it must be a high quality product.' Besides, it is on sale at a reduced price.

Consumer A seems to fit in a different time-frame from consumer B. In fact, consumer A seems to belong to the post-war period, and consumer B seems to belong to a younger generation. For consumer A, it is possible to identify surplus value and to experience it. Consumer B experiences only difficulties in assessing product quality and price–quality relationships. For him, buying is like guessing. Although the contrast has been exaggerated, the observation of consumer behaviour in present-day markets reveals that 'modern' consumers have difficulty in understanding information and making well-judged choices. The first, tentative conclusion we want to draw is that our definition of marketing does not seem to apply any longer to many consumers in Western economies. In fact, there may not be surplus value because all options can be positioned in a very narrow quality range; or there is surplus value, but it is not experienced.

While consumer B seems to look more like the contemporary consumer than consumer A, we feel that consumer A is often taken as the prototype in marketing decisions. Expressed in a bold proposition, this would mean that marketing continues to address a type of consumer that no longer exists. While marketing is focused on the production of surplus value, surplus value is no longer experienced. Marketing may thus be violating its own definition (Sheth and Sisodia, 1997).

Context developments

In the following section, we want to discuss the validity of our proposition. We will present an inventory of the developments that we feel affect the nature of marketing. The developments will be briefly discussed in random order. One of the noteworthy changes in the past century has been the growing impact of *technology* (Davis and Meyer, 1998). The benefits for consumers have been enormous. New products and services became available, and the quality of existing products increased dramatically. The relentless search for higher quality resulted in the reduction of poor products, and narrowed the quality range. In comparative product tests of consumer organizations poor products are seldom found nowadays. Generally speaking, products and services do not differ considerably in their high level of quality. What is more, quality problems tend to be backed up by warranties and guarantees. We should note, however, that the high level of quality and the relatively small quality differences among products do not urge and motivate consumers to engage in elaborate quality comparisons. The motivation to do so is also affected by the affluence that characterizes most Western consumers. To the extent that there is the risk of a bad buy, this risk can be easily taken for most products. In the occasion of a real disappointment, the consumer has the financial means to simply purchase another product.

Technology has had effects beyond products, services and their quality. New interactive media such as the Internet were created with information technology. Communication is not limited any more by geographical and time boundaries. The Internet is the ultimate example of a medium that allows for almost unlimited information exchange. While the abundance of information seems to facilitate careful and elaborate pre-purchase comparisons, the very amount of information itself seems to block information processing. The phenomenon of information overload is well-known. Even if consumers are motivated to acquire information about purchase options, they may be so overwhelmed by information that the actual use of information is limited. By the introduction of Internet and other technologically sophisticated media such as cellular phones, new distribution possibilities have opened up. There are many different ways in which companies may contact their clientele and potential buyers.

Both technological and economic developments resulted in an expansion of international marketing. Competition is often so fierce on national markets that companies look for new freedom to manoeuvre on foreign markets. Differences in prices for primary resources such as labour result in new market opportunities. These, in turn, boost competition to an even higher level. For consumers, the market supply is abundant and also constantly changing.

Marketing spirals

Our conclusion is that competition is growing continuously and at an ever-increasing pace, and that the supply side is constantly introducing new products, services and instruments to deliver (surplus) value to consumers. This development may outgrow consumers and their limitations. The gap between offered and experienced surplus value is widening. This may be illustrated by four circular developments: the 'innovation spiral', the 'communication spiral', the 'distribution spiral' and the 'price spiral', together with the overall 'marketing spiral' (Poiesz and van Raaij, 2002).

The innovation spiral describes how the need for surplus value leads to the frantic introduction of new products, resulting in an overload of 'newness' in the market which, in fact, reduces the visibility of an innovation. This stimulates the search for other new products, and so on.

The other spirals demonstrate a similar process. The communication spiral, for example, suggests that the collective need to be (more) visible in highly competitive markets cumulates into an information overload that reduces the impact of individual messages or campaigns. In turn, this again increases the need to communicate. New media seem to provide a relief from the information overload and the competition for consumer attention, but this relief is only temporary. Communicators imitate each other and adopt each newly available medium in a short time.

If consumers cannot be reached by communication, they will have to be contacted directly (e.g., by direct mail or telephone). Also, for the instrument of distribution, the circular spiral phenomenon can be observed. There is a high need to contact consumers. On the aggregate level, this results in a 'contact overload', which ultimately reduces the frequency or quality of contacts, so that the need to contact is increased even further.

If it becomes more difficult to generate (the experience of) surplus value with the previous instruments, consumers become less willing to pay higher prices. Companies are forced to lower their prices to stay in business. This reduces their investments and, consequently, the possibility to generate surplus value. Prices need then to be lowered even further.

We may combine these four spirals in an overall marketing spiral, as shown in Figure 3.1. The marketing spiral illustrates the struggle for surplus value. The spiral effect is due to the inability of consumers to keep track of marketing progress. If marketing is defined as the process to generate experienced surplus value for all parties involved, the marketing spiral shows how this definition does not seem to apply any more to markets of Western economies. The marketing paradigm needs to be overhauled or replaced.

We discussed our views with about 200 marketing managers in the Netherlands. They feel the growing pressure of competition, and

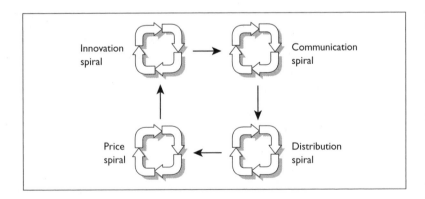

Figure 3.1   The marketing spirals

they experience the reduced effectiveness of the traditional marketing instruments. Even though there is still confidence in these instruments, there is also growing concern. A reconsideration of the marketing paradigm is called for. We will make an inventory of possible escape routes from the marketing spiral and use these for presenting a future marketing scenario. Of course, while the escape routes are being tried already in contemporary marketing, the future scenario is hypothetical by definition. Also, if the scenario were to materialize at all, we do not know whether this would happen within the suggested time-frame of five years. We feel confident, however, that within this period new initiatives towards the scenario will develop.

How to escape?

What escape routes are being developed that cannot be categorized as mere variations of existing marketing instruments, but as paradigmatic developments? We identify two very general avenues. Both can be taken as a return to the core meaning of marketing: namely, an increasing customer focus, and the recovery of value. Today, many companies present themselves as customer oriented. They realize that, ultimately, marketing can only be successful if the consumer is given a central position. Part of this is the *individualization* trend: the growing need for consumers to have products and services adapted to their own idiosyncratic characteristics and preferences. Also, they reconsider the uniqueness of the contribution they are making. Usually, the surplus value was defined in an objective, technological sense. More and more, the emphasis shifts towards the subjective notion of surplus value. We also move away from the transaction as the creation of value to usage value. Products and services do not create value at their purchase but at their usage. The product or service *experience* itself becomes the focus of interest. Products and services may then be viewed as instrumental and necessary conditions for the experience (Pine and Gilmore, 1999). The other trend is the growing attention to *customer values* as such (see Scott, 1998). Over time, companies show a tendency to position their products and services at a higher level in the benefit hierarchy (Reynolds and Gutman, 1984). At the lowest levels, benefits relate to concrete functional effects. At the highest level, benefits relate to the association with general values such as friendship, peace, safety, and an exciting life. Companies attempt to claim these higher values, which are limited in number (Rokeach, 1973; Schwartz and Bilsky, 1987, 1990), in order to use them as an umbrella for marketing and communication activities.

What can companies do to address both individualization and experienced value creation? We see three levels at which this may be done: the operational, tactical and strategic level. By definition, the operational level is associated with measures that have an impact in the short run and that may be easily copied by the competition. This is less true for the tactical level. Policy measures at the strategic level often take longer to materialize, have a long life cycle, and are less easily adopted by competitors. We see activities at each of these levels.

At the operational level, companies use psychological insights to accommodate the trends of individualization and customer value. They use market research to find out why consumers do or do not buy/use available products and services. There is a growing interest in acquiring a deeper insight in consumer behaviour. This leads to fine-tuning of existing marketing instruments. If a policy proves to be successful, it may almost immediately be adopted by competitors. Therefore, operational measures do not provide an escape from the marketing spiral.

At the tactical level, the question of value for particular customers leads to the use of customer relationship management (CRM) systems, the integration of products and services to generate new value, the integration of communication media, the matching of distribution channels and the application of dual pricing. Each of these instruments contributes to an increase of the value experienced by the consumer, and to a long-term relationship with the customer. These measures result in a revitalization of value, but can be copied by competing suppliers. In this sense, they allow only for a temporary escape from the marketing spiral.

It is argued here that a more definite exit from the marketing spiral may be achieved by a particular strategic approach. This approach is different from the existing measures in two different ways. First, it consists of a combination of strategies. Second, it is only possible with the support of information and communication technology (ICT). In fact, ICT will serve as the backbone to the hybrid strategy that we propose. This strategy will lead to the future scenario that we will present as the ultimate marketing scenario. Here, the marketing spiral will only turn to the benefit of the parties concerned; there will be no detrimental effects. Marketing will not suffocate itself. In fact, in the future scenario, the marketing spiral will run the other way around, resulting in a constant improvement of the experienced surplus value, to the benefit of both parties involved.

We will first construct this scenario with the help of an extrapolation of current developments, and then we will point to the crucial role of ICT. When discussing the tactical measures, two developments have already been noted that seem to be particularly important for reasons to be explained. One is the *integration of products and services*; the other one is the growing emphasis on *long-term relationships* of suppliers and customers. Both developments will be described in terms of four distinct phases.

Integration of products and services

Integration of products and services will probably develop according to the following four stages:

Stage 1: At this stage there is a complete lack of integration. In fact, products and services are presented on a stand-alone basis. No additional benefits are attached to products, often not even a systematic branding. Products and services are presented as they are.

Stage 2: This is the phase of the 'augmented' products and services. The original product or service is combined with additional benefits that traditionally did not belong to that product or service (e.g., a car is sold with a lease contract). Other examples include a washing machine for which an extended service guarantee can be purchased, or new subscribers to a magazine may be entitled to a rebate when visiting an amusement park.

Stage 3: Products and services that originally were marketed as independent goods are now combined to provide additional value. A television set is integrated with a video recorder. A video camera and photo camera are combined in a single device. Financial products are combined so that mortgages, insurances, pension plans, investments and loans belong to one integrated all-in financial package. In this phase we want to refer to an integrated domain package, as the products and services belong to the same category or domain (e.g., photography, finances). The value is here in the mutual adaptation of the elements of the set. Note that we do not refer to mere cross-selling, but to a package that is better than the sum of its parts.

Stage 4: Products and services of different domains are combined into functional packages. New packages are formed that are inconceivable in traditional top-down marketing, but are very functional in a bottom-up marketing approach. Consumers interested in living comfortably, for example, are not interested in a house only, but also in interior decoration, garden architecture and maintenance, house repairs and cleaning, and safety and monitoring during absence. The transport of children to and from schools, sports clubs and discos may be part of the package. The example seems to be far-fetched, but reflects a different way of thinking about consumer needs or, for that matter, experienced surplus value.

These four stages show that single products become part of a cross-domain package of products and services. The provider of this package then becomes the trusted brand for a group of loyal customers. This trusted brand adapts the product package to the plans, desires and capabilities of individual customers to prevent and solve problems and to increase the satisfaction and well-being of these individual customers.

Customer relationships

The other development concerns the growing attention to long-term customer relationships. Also here we may identify four different phases that point to different stages in the development. Customer relationships will probably develop according to the following four stages:

Stage 1: There is no relationship between the product/service provider and the customer. The company (the market supplier) is not interested in the next purchase. A single transaction suffices. The company does not bother about whether the transactions can be attributed to initial or repeat purchases.

Stage 2: There is a short-term relationship of supplier and customer. There is an interest in persuading consumers to return for the next purchase. The time perspective is still short, however.

Stage 3: The company develops a loyalty programme (bonus card, airmiles) with the intention of stimulating repeat purchases and customer commitment (Butscher, 2002).

Stage 4: In this phase the company strives for a relationship that covers a life-time. Customers are followed over different life stages, and the products and services that are provided are carefully attuned to these subsequent stages.

Note that CRM as it is practised today is largely producer oriented. Present-day CRM is mainly an optimization of the seller–retailer–buyer channel to get an efficient flow of products and information through the channel. CRM is mainly channel management rather than customer management.

In these four stages, the duration and intensity of the relationship grows. The trust between the supplying company or 'brand' and the customer also increases. When mutual trust has developed between supplier and customer, parties are willing to provide more information to each other to increase their mutual benefit.

The value matrix

As indicated before, for both tendencies we already see initiatives in the market. We have also noted that measures relating to these tendencies individually run the risk of being copied, so that the company is pulled back into the marketing spiral. Therefore we propose to combine the two tendencies, resulting in a strong hybrid strategy where the increasing product sophistication is made possible by long-term customer relationships, and where the long-term customer relationships are supported by product sophistication. In fact, it may not be possible for one development to enter a next stage without the other development entering the next stage as well. The two developments are mutually supporting and should keep each other in balance. Individual customization of products and services only pays off in a long-term relationship. It is argued here that experienced surplus value can only be realized over time by the combination of these developments. Referring to the issue of the marketing paradigm, we feel that the current paradigm consists of a plethora of individual activities, each trying independently to create or support surplus value. The (financial) energy to do this is fragmented and spreads in all possible directions. A change of paradigm would involve a stronger focus on synergies, and a return to the essence of marketing.

The combination of the two developments may be illustrated in a matrix that we call the 'value matrix' (Figure 3.2) (Poiesz and van Raaij, 2002). If both developments occur in the same speed, the actual development will take place along the value diagonal.

With regard to the value matrix shown in Figure 3.2, the following propositions can be stated (see overleaf).

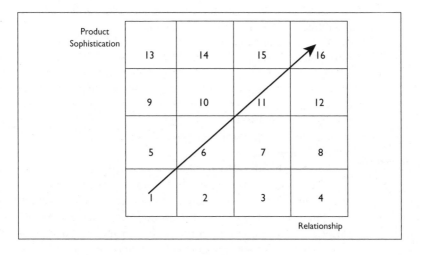

Figure 3.2 The value matrix

1   The two axes of the matrix are mutually supporting. The development of long-term relationships is not possible without simultaneously expanding the notion of value. Vice versa, it is impossible to build larger product/service packages without being able to count on long-term customer relationships: it is simply economically inconceivable.

2   The first proposition implies that the optimal strategy for a company is the diagonal. Therefore, we call this the 'value diagonal'. A deviation is possible, and may even be effective, but is likely to be very inefficient. For example, if a company attempts to increase the duration of the relationship without offering additional value, the company will have to pay the consumer to stay. This is what is in fact happening with many bonus programmes. Consumers have to be 'bribed' into a long-term relationship. Such programmes symbolize the desperation of marketing policy-makers. For the same reason, CRM systems are no substitute, in themselves, for a lack of customer value. The matrix shows how companies may follow different routes to different positions, but also that it may be worthwhile to migrate towards the diagonal and then follow it.

3   As implied by the first two propositions, the ultimate marketing situation is cell 16. This is the future scenario that we were aiming for. This is an optimal marketing situation for several reasons.

   (a)   The consumer is unwilling to show switching behaviour because he has experienced all kinds of benefits; the provider, of course, does not want the customer to leave. Organizational planning is much supported. Marketing funds do not have to be spent on mass media, but can be fine-tuned for the benefit of individual consumers. Cost effectiveness is very high.

   (b)   The consumer has developed a high trust in the provider. As a result, he is more than willing to give elaborate feedback on consumption experiences. The provider can use this to increase the size and quality of the presented package, and to use the information for similar consumers. This type of information is returned, of course.

   (c)   The provider has developed extensive knowledge about the individual consumer, allowing the former to suggest new products and services that are most likely to lead to very high satisfaction.

   (d)   The interests of both provider and consumer run completely parallel. There is no room or reason for the traditional antagonism that still characterizes market systems now.

   (e)   In cell 16 (Figure 3.2), market power is very high because, once a relationship with a customer has been established, it becomes almost invulnerable. Switching costs and opportunity costs are very high for parties that want to leave or to switch.

(f) With long-term relationships with providers of sets of integrated products and services, there is no need for a large variety of different brands. The number of providers that is in direct contact with customers is low relative to the present number. Market power will be redistributed, so that most power is reallocated to the party (brand) closest to the consumer. In fact, that party may be viewed as having the mandate to serve as a representative, bargaining with a variety of producers on behalf of large consumer groups.

(g) It may be expected that the long-term relationships, based on commitment and not on bribes, will result in the formation of clubs or communities around a provider brand (Butscher, 2002).

4 The value matrix may result in the reformulation of customer needs, customer values and surplus customer value. These are unlikely to be structured according to the traditional division of markets into profit, non-profit and government sectors. Rather, it may be expected that the boundaries between these sectors will gradually fade away.

Information and communication technology

These developments are not possible without the use of ICT. In ICT, four stages of development and application may be distinguished:

Stage 1: In the first stage, ICT was used to make present processes and procedures more efficient. Product scanning at checkout counters of supermarkets made checking out more efficient than before and the queues are now shorter.

Stage 2: In the second phase, customer data (names, addresses, purchases) are stored in databases and customers may be tracked and addressed individually. In contacts with customers the salesperson now has the information about the customer readily available. This makes personal contacts and personal selling more effective and more 'personal'. At this stage, salespersons may use the database to contact customers more frequently in order to sell more. This is a danger because the 'contact spiral' may start to spin and may cause adverse effects on consumers.

Stage 3: Now, ICT and, in particular, the Internet are information sources for both suppliers and customers. With the Internet, the power shifts from retailers to consumers. Consumers may use intelligent search agents to retrieve relevant information from the web and to compare these options. Knowledge bots (Ask Jeeves!), search bots (Katipo), shopping bots (Bottom Dollar) or communication bots (ALife Messenger) can be employed. Intelligent search agents will ultimately be programmed with customer desires and plans, and will find solutions to problems. Thus search costs have diminished dramatically. If agents carefully select relevant information, the communication spiral may be avoided.

Stage 4: In the future, ICT will take a more proactive stand. The agent becomes an assistant with a profound knowledge of his 'boss', the consumer. The agent assists the consumer with relevant information and alerts the consumer about deadlines. Areas of agent assistance are: information management, financial management, contract management, optimization of travel routes, time and agenda management, workflow management, recreation management, negotiation management, purchasing and selling products. Other agents serve suppliers and select optimal points to provide customers with 'customized' information and services.

ICT will thus play a crucial role in the future symbiosis and interaction of suppliers and customers. Agents may continuously monitor the situation of the customer and find improvements to increase the satisfaction and well-being of the customers. Agents learn from the feedback they get from customers to improve their services. Combinations of products and services are continuously tested and improved. Trade-offs are made between short-term and long-term benefits of purchases and investments.

In stage 4 and cell 16 of Figure 3.2, products and services are no longer evaluated on their separate benefits, but on their contributions to the total (mega) package and thus on their contribution to the well-being of 'their' members (customers). The ultimate objective of marketing is not to sell products, but to increase the well-being of customers.

Conclusions

The start of the 21st century has been accompanied by a growing concern about the gradually accelerating reduction of the effectiveness of traditional marketing instruments. In marketing, the high intensity of competition has led to a rapidly increasing growth of the quantity and quality of marketing measures. Traditional marketing is turning into a self-suffocating phenomenon. It approaches the situation where benefits are balanced by costs. Old certainties are replaced by new risks. Added value – to us the very essence of the marketing concept – is under pressure. We conclude, therefore, that the concept of added value needs to be redefined.

As the density problem is located at the operational and tactical levels of marketing, the strategic level is the only level where, in the future, added value can be defined. Added value is now an ad hoc, unidimensional and manufacturer-defined concept. It will have to change into a long-term, multidimensional and consumer-defined concept. Single products and services cannot be held capable of creating value at the strategic level. Therefore they will have to team up, and will have to combine their respective functions into synergy-based value.

We conclude that marketing will have to demonstrate a growing willingness to merge products/services into an integrated package for the benefit of consumers. This is not the same as merging companies for this serves only to increase market effectiveness and marketing efficiencies. Merging products/services is intended to increase the value experienced by the consumer. This will require a reconsideration of the supply side at the micro and macro level. Exactly how packages will be formed strongly depends upon the initiatives of highly reputable parties on the market supply side.

We expect that the initial reluctance of consumers to give information (privacy) and to delegate decisions (independence) will be replaced by a growing willingness to do so. Gradually, over time, consumers will experience the added value that is the result of the decisions that have been made for them (high quality outcomes, no loss of time and effort). Perceived risk will be reduced and, gradually, the request to provide support in consumption decisions will be expanded.

These new developments that we anticipate will change the face of marketing. As the effectiveness of marketing measures is reduced, so is the likelihood of their being deployed in the future. Traditional (mass marketing) instruments will gradually fade from existence. More time and effort will be spent on contacts with individual consumers. Quantitatively and qualitatively, these contacts will have to be set at the level where they will be accepted by the individual consumer.

For two reasons, the number of brands will be reduced dramatically. First, the added value of individual products and services will depend on their particular contribution to the larger packages. The function of brands will be transferred to the organizer of these packages so that the organizer acquires the status of brand. Mass communication is not functional any longer, as consumers will not select their own brands. In sum, marketing will be turned upside-down. To some extent, these developments are scary as it is not clear where, when and how it will start. On the other hand, it will force marketing to return to its original mission: the creation of added value for customers.

Our last conclusion is that we cannot predict the future; nobody can. What we have done, however, is to use insights derived from recent and current developments and extrapolate these into the future. This is, of course, highly risky. On the other hand, examples of the effects we predict are cropping up in real life markets. The impossibility of predicting the future implies that it is not yet possible to assess the validity of the presented arguments. For now, we can only keep our eyes open and call for further discussion. The area of marketing is too important and too interesting to have it surprise us.

Knowledge transfer through marketing textbooks: the Howard and Sheth buyer behaviour typology as a case in point

walter van waterschoot and
els gilbrecht[*]

Introduction

The principal argument of this chapter is that a managerial discipline such as marketing should not generate knowledge merely to satisfy intellectual scholarly appetites. Ultimately, knowledge should be *usable* and *applicable* in particular contextual circumstances. Application of knowledge presupposes that it is transferred to ultimate users in an appropriate fashion, through appropriate vehicles. Critically appraising this overall communication process of knowledge, as well as particular aspects of that process, is therefore not a luxury afforded to academic intellectuals. One such major aspect of critical appraisal concerns the very building blocks of the marketing discipline. By this are meant fundamental concepts and typologies which are perceived as vital inputs for professional practice and more advanced study, and which for that reason are conveyed to almost any student or practitioner of the discipline. Two easy and evident examples are, of course, the marketing concept and the marketing mix classification.

[*] The authors would like to thank Piet Vanden Abeele (Catholic University of Leuven) and Christophe Van den Bulte (the Wharton School) for their critical comments, and Marleen van Waterschoot for a revision of the English.

Apart from summarizing and representing the elementary, formalized knowledge of the discipline, building blocks play a more complex role:

1   They serve as components, stepping stones, or frameworks for new conceptual and other developments.

2   They provide a frame of reference for conveying results from applied and scientific empirical research to receivers and potential users. If the discipline's building blocks are to serve as reliable expedients of advanced scientific and applied knowledge, a first and minimal requirement is that they themselves are correctly conveyed to end-users.

Marketing textbooks and academic aspirations

A major source of information to judge knowledge transfer are published marketing textbooks. They represent visible, accessible, and therefore verifiable vehicles in the communication process of marketing knowledge. They typically contain crystallized knowledge, often distilled from more scientifically oriented sources such marketing journals. In textbook form, presumably, they are most likely to reach the discipline's ultimate users such as students, managers and teachers. Academic authors, then, should have high aspirations to incorporate adequate conceptual and practical information in textbooks in the most appropriate ways, and many strive to achieve this.

One simple assumption is that textbooks do succeed in transferring marketing knowledge concerning the discipline's basic building blocks in a satisfactory manner to potential users. The alternative hypothesis is that this communication process is not without problems and may be in need of improvement. This is much more challenging and worthy of investigation. The alternative hypothesis fits more readily into a marketing discipline that is open to self-criticism, ever-ready to improve, and concerned about phenomena that hamper knowledge dissemination. Indeed, the beginning of a new century is a psychologically unique moment for such a critical perspective and appraisal, and hence our participation in this book.

As always, however, there is a problem, for studying the quality of the discipline's knowledge transfer is a potentially titanic job, as superficiality in communication cannot be deduced from superficial analysis. Indications derived from a thorough study of a single, but well-known and accepted, case will therefore be more reliable than conclusions based on 'scratching the surface' of numerous cases. For that reason, we concentrate our attention on the Howard and Sheth typology of buyer behaviour as a case in point. While many other choices of single cases were possible, we judged the Howard and Sheth case to be well suited for this purpose for several reasons. Buyer behaviour in general is one of the more important subfields in marketing. Different types of buying behaviour dramatically affect the relevance and irrelevance of practical marketing approaches. The Howard and Sheth typology, in particular, is still one of the seminal and most accepted typologies in this subfield. It serves as an important expedient for the transfer of applied and fundamental findings. Last but not least, the typology is not so straightforward that nothing could go wrong in the communication process.

The following section of the chapter concentrates on practitioners' expectations of textbooks in general and buyer behaviour typologies in particular. The next section summarizes Howard and Sheth's typology as put forward by the authors in their original contributions. Then, the research approach is outlined. In the next section, findings of a content analysis of Howard and Sheth's descriptions are summarized. This section assesses the criteria by which Howard and Sheth descriptions differ from the original typology, as well as the relative occurrence of biased versus non-biased versions. This section also contains some indications on the relative popularity of the Howard and Sheth typology amongst buyer behaviour classifications and on the way it is presented. The subsequent section examines the reasons behind the diversity of descriptions encountered, and indicates some negative implications. This is followed by a discussion on some of the positive consequences of observed inaccuracies. The chapter continues with an assessment from the point of view of practitioners. The last section adopts a broader academic perspective, and provides conclusions for the overall discipline in terms of a critical 21st-century perspective.

Practitioners' expectations about marketing textbooks

In more than any other business or managerial discipline, it is particularly important to assess the actual performance of marketing textbooks as seen by practitioners, not only because practitioners are driven by bottom-line imperatives, but also because of differences in personality and professional scenarios, informational needs, and in the ways those needs are resolved. Even so, some common characteristics can be identified that bear on the implications of this chapter.

Practitioners rely on multiple sources to satisfy information needs, ranging from printed, electronic and personal media, and from public to private media. The mixture of these sources is shaped by typical aims and constraints following from the professional framework in which these executives are located. Usually, time is a significant resource constraint. Managerial energy put into listening, watching or reading needs to pay off rapidly. Statistical juggling and academic theorizing are not what practitioners want or need. In their selection of printed resources, practitioners typically turn to sources considered both relevant and readable, such as business magazines and textbooks. In the textbooks, they would expect to find reliable relevant state-of-the-art scenarios, conveyed in highly readable and interest-provoking ways, and containing a wealth of practical and applicable findings derived from recent cutting-edge research. Whether they find this, however, is debatable.

Taking buyer behaviour as a case in point, for managers in search of information on buyer behaviour typologies, general textbook expectations will translate into a set of specific requirements such as:

- meaningful labelling
- similarity in sources
- relative importance of different typologies
- reliable discussion of consequences

A first and logical requirement is that meaningful labels be used to denote the core concepts in a typology, and that these labels are clearly defined and their specific and relevant behavioural aspects explicitly described. Second, practitioners would expect accepted knowledge on established typologies to be referred to in a similar fashion in different (textbook) sources, using uniform labels and label descriptions across these sources. If several typologies have been developed – as is the case for buying behaviour – or if a given typology has evolved over time, they would be interested in similarities, differences and additional insights gained from the different typologies or subsequent elaborations. Third, practitioners would value indications on the relative importance of the different behavioural types within a typology or across typologies, indicating what are dominant behaviours, but also where exceptions lie. Last but not least, managers would hope to be offered a reliable, thorough discussion of the instrumental, tactical and strategic consequences of the foregoing.

The essence of the Howard and Sheth buyer behaviour typology: a stage classification

The Howard and Sheth typology is a deductive typology, distinguishing between three types of buying situations called Extensive Problem Solving (EPS), Limited Problem Solving (LPS) and Routinised Response Behaviour (RRB). It is derived from theory rather than based on a pragmatic grouping of occasional elements encountered in reality. It classifies buying situations in a sequential manner, more particularly as three stages of a buying process. Table 4.1 provides formal definitions from the principal publication of the typology by Howard and Sheth (1969) and by Howard (1989). Analysis of the category descriptions leaves no doubt as to the stage character of the Howard and Sheth classification. The definitions clearly present the three types of decision situations as subsequent stages in a buying process. The same holds for the wording, phrasing and explanations in the main publication (Howard and Sheth, 1969, pp. 27–8, 46–7, 49, 188, 404, 418). Earlier as well as later publications by Howard and/or Sheth confirm this stage idea, or at least never disconfirm it (Howard, 1963, 1974, 1977 and 1989; Howard and Sheth, 1967, 1969).

The Howard and Sheth typology is part of a comprehensive theory of buying behaviour. Its process view rests on a number of assumptions, including assumptions with regard to the quantity and quality of search and intellectual effort. In particular, the typology assumes that the amount of effort gradually decreases as the buying process evolves. Differences in effort go together with subsequent buying stages, in the sense that they supposedly follow from the nature of these stages. If an individual shifts from EPS to LPS, for example, search efforts are assumed to diminish. Two elements are apparent from the publications of Howard and Sheth: first, Howard and Sheth postulate a causal link between stage and effort; and second, they imply a specific direction for this causality. Stage is the explanatory element and the magnitude of effort follows from it. In other words, the effort assumption inherent to the Howard and Sheth typology is of a subordinate, secondary nature. The predominant classificatory basis consists of stages. Another remarkable trait of the Howard and Sheth typology and theory is the 'homogeneity assumption'. Differences between products are treated as exogenous factors 'outside' the theory (Howard and Sheth, 1969, p. 68). They affect the number of brands a buyer considers (p. 74) as well as the overall amount of search (Howard and Sheth, 1969, p. 322), but are neither part of the definitions nor of the descriptions of the EPS, LPS and

Table 4.1 Formal definitions of the categories of the Howard and Sheth typology

Formal definitions	Howard and Sheth (1969), p. 27	Howard and Sheth (1969), p. 418	Howard (1989), pp. 361–4
Extensive Problem Solving	'refers to the early stages of repetitive decision making, in which the buyer has not yet developed well-defined and structured choice criteria. The buyer has no strong predispositions towards any of the brands he is considering as alternatives'	'the buyer does not have well-formed choice criteria and does not have a product class concept. He needs information to provide the basis for forming his choice criteria, and correspondingly he has very limited preference (attitude) for any one brand'	'Buying behaviour exhibited by consumers who are buying an unfamiliar category of brand. It is characterised typically by the need for substantial information and time to choose because the consumer must form a concept of a new category'
Limited Problem Solving	'is the next stage, in which the choice criteria are well-defined and structured but the buyer is undecided about which of a set of brands is best for him. The buyer has moderately high predispositions towards a number of brands, but does not have very strong preference for any one brand'	'the buyer has well-formed choice criteria, hence a well-defined product class concept. His attitude, though positive toward brands in his evoked set, is not strongly favourable to any one brand because his information to judge one of them is inadequate'	'Buying behaviour exhibited by consumers buying a new brand in a familiar category. It is typically characterised by considerable information seeking and time to choose'
Routinised Response Behaviour	'is the last stage, in which the buyer not only has well-defined and structured choice criteria, but also strong predisposition toward one brand. At this stage, although the buyer may consider several brands as possible alternatives, he has in fact, only one or two brands in mind as the most probable choice alternatives'	'the buyer is not only very familiar with the product class but with all brands in his evoked set so that the only information that he needs has to do with the value of the inhibitors that constitute his purchasing plan which underlies his intention. The buyer has a definite preference for one brand over other brands in his evoked set'	'Buying behaviour characterised by consumers buying a brand they have bought before. It is typically characterised by little or no information seeking and is performed quickly'

RRB concepts. The three buying types are defined as if they were equally representative for all sorts of products.

The research method: content analysis

To formally analyse how the Howard and Sheth typology is reproduced in marketing textbooks, a content analysis procedure is adopted (Kassarjian, 1977; Kassarjian and Healy, 1983). The study population here consists of general marketing textbooks (both introductory and more advanced) as well as buyer behaviour textbooks. The sample comprises all English marketing textbooks of this kind available in the library of the authors' university and published after the 'official' introduction of the Howard and Sheth typology in 1969. The convenient nature of the sample fits the aim of the study. The study intends to investigate *whether there exists a problem of inaccurate and incomplete transfer of knowledge in marketing.* While the sample slightly overemphasizes recent editions, which are more likely to distort the content of the original Howard and Sheth publication, it still contains a number of older publications. At the same time, as a result of the library's selective ordering policy, the sample bias is in favour of established, high quality books, which are expected to be more careful in the way they formulate and reproduce marketing information.

The elements studied in the content analysis are the dimensions associated with the Howard and Sheth typology, and whether or not these dimensions are entangled. A pilot study based on a subsample of textbooks identifies up to three 'dimensions' in the Howard and Sheth descriptions, as listed below:

1   A stage dimension, similar to the formal definitions by Howard and Sheth. An illustrative statement is the following: *'The other type of problem solving behaviour (routinised response behaviour) exists when the consumer knows both the criteria to be used and how various brands rate on these criteria'* (Zaltman and Wallendorf, 1983, p. 629).

2   A dimension indicating the amount of search effort. An illustrative statement is the following: *'On a continuum of effort ranging from very high to very low, we can distinguish three specific levels of consumer decision making: extensive problem solving, limited problem solving, and routinised response behaviour'* (Schiffman and Kanuk, 1994, p. 565).

3   A dimension for the importance of product categories. An illustrative statement is the following: '*This automatic or routinised response behaviour is more typical in repeat purchases of convenience goods, such as toothpaste or laundry detergent*' (Zaltman and Wallendorf, 1983, p. 629).

The pilot study also revealed that if more than one dimension is present in Howard and Sheth's discussions, these dimensions are sometimes 'intertwined' or 'entangled'. Presence of 'entanglement' forms the fourth attribute in the content analysis. In the 'no entanglement' case, the dimensions are treated as conceptually or theoretically independent, yet may be factually correlated (see Figure 4.1a). While each level on a given dimension (e.g., little experience) could in principle be combined with any level on another dimension (e.g., low/high search effort or involvement), some combinations are presented as being more likely than others. In line with this, a 'no entanglement' discussion formulates descriptions, definitions and explanations in terms of relative frequency or 'likelihood' of occurrence. An illustrative statement is:

> *In general*, product classes in which there are many alternatives that are expensive, complex, or new will require the consumer to collect more information and take longer to make a purchase decision. For example, buying an automobile is *probably* one of the most difficult purchase decisions most consumers make ... Such a decision will *usually* require extensive information search and time before a decision is made. (Tarpey, Donnelly and Peter, 1979, p. 53; emphasis added)

An 'entangled' discussion treats the dimensions as if they naturally occur together or follow the one from the other, without leaving room for other coincidences or sequences (see Figure 4.1b). It overgeneralizes what is encountered in the majority of cases, providing strongly affirmative and absolute descriptions of prototypical cases. The following quotation is illustrative:

> Finally, some product classes require what is called routinised decision making. For these product classes, such as cigarettes or some food products, the consumer has faced the decision many times before and has found an acceptable alternative. Thus, little or no information is collected and the consumer purchases in an habitual, automatic manner. (Tarpey, Donnelly and Peter, 1979, p. 54)

The degree to which an Howard and Sheth description contains a stage aspect, an effort aspect and an importance aspect is measured by means of a five-point rating scale, indicating whether a particular

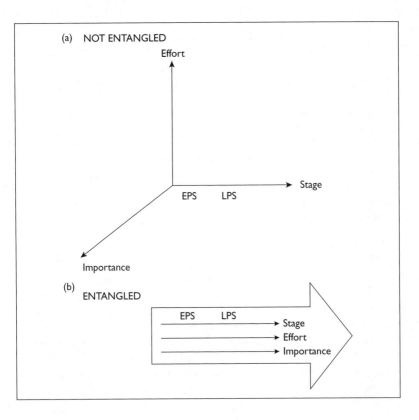

Figure 4.1   Graphical representation of a three-dimensional
Howard and Sheth discussion

dimension is 'very strongly', 'strongly', 'moderately', 'hardly', or 'not at all' present. The ratings for the three dimensions also allow the identification of the one most prominently referred to in a text. The latter is said to 'dominate' the description. To assess the presence of 'entanglement', a five-point scale turned out to be too refined, and only two classes were retained: 'entangled' versus 'not entangled'.

The content analysis is carried out by a jury consisting of two experts in a stepwise fashion. In a first step, each expert studies and evaluates the texts independently and repeatedly. In a next step, the evaluations from the two experts are cross-validated. As shown in Table 4.2, both intra-judge and inter-judge reliability are quite satisfactory. Note that, compared to the stage and involvement dimensions, inter-judge correlations for the effort dimension are somewhat lower. This follows from the fact

Table 4.2   Overview of reliability scores

Intra-judge reliability		
Proportion of cases for which identical results are obtained after:	Expert 1	Expert 2
First control round	0.70	0.43
Second control round	0.20	0.45
Third control round	0.10	0.12
Inter-judge reliability		
	Attributes	Reliability
Number of dimensions included		0.95*
Degree of presence of	Stage	0.88†
included dimensions	Effort	0.73*
	Involvement	0.93†
Dominance of included dimensions		0.73*
Entanglement of dimensions		0.73*

* % of cases in which experts agree; † correlation coefficient between ratings.

that a number of text fragments are internally inconsistent. They emphasize effort in some text parts or category descriptions, but not in others. The lower reliability for the effort scores leads to some disagreement in terms of dominance, which is almost exclusively caused by (minor) judgement differences between stage and stage-effort dominated, or between effort and stage-effort dominated situations. For these few situations where expert opinions are not exactly the same, a 'discussion round' is organized leading to a consensus between the two experts on all aspects and for all texts considered.

The (degree of) presence of the stage, effort and involvement dimensions, and their entanglement, constitute the core of the content analysis; yet, for reasons of completeness, attention is also paid to the popularity and presentation of the Howard and Sheth classification. To assess the relative popularity of the Howard and Sheth typology, the presence or absence of other buying behaviour typologies alongside Howard and Sheth's is recorded. In terms of presentation, attention is paid to the length of Howard and Sheth's discussions, and the use of quotations and formal references.

Findings from the study: contents of the Howard and Sheth discussions

Of 127 sampled textbooks, 37 present a discussion of the Howard and Sheth classification (31 if Howard and Sheth controlled sources are left out) generating 40 descriptions of the Howard and Sheth typology. The sample shows a large diversity. Based on the number and kind of dimensions included as well as on their dominance, 16 possible types of descriptions can be distinguished. Of these, seven are actually present in the sample. Moreover, even within each of these types, the relative importance of the dimensions varies. In summary, very few cases in the sample are completely alike.

It is important to keep in mind that the formal definitions of Howard and Sheth are of a one-dimensional (stage) nature. They are taken up and rated in Table 4.3 to serve as a point of comparison. *A stunning observation is that not one single textbook contains a discussion that exactly matches these definitions. Particularly amazing is that all descriptions other than the formal Howard and Sheth definitions are multidimensional instead of one-dimensional.*

The two-dimensional stage-dominated type of description is most frequently encountered in textbooks written or edited by Howard and/or Sheth themselves. These texts explicitly incorporate the 'effort assumption' of their stage typology in the description, which therefore become of a two-dimensional nature. But if sources controlled by Howard and Sheth are left out, only three cases remain where stage and effort are present, and where stage then dominates. In other words, only three textbooks in the sample not controlled by Howard and Sheth provide discussions that closely resemble the 1969 descriptions by the original authors. Next to these, the sample contains only two more two-dimensional cases, both of which are of the stage-effort-dominated type.

Remarkably, the majority of all cases, or 25 out of 40, are of a three-dimensional nature. If sources controlled by Howard and/or Sheth themselves are left out, this figure rises to about 80 per cent (24 out of 31). The stage aspect is always present. However, if Howard and Sheth controlled sources are left out, it is dominant (alone or together with another dimension) in only 15 out of 31 cases. The effort aspect, on the other hand, is present in all the discussions of the sample except in the formal Howard and Sheth definitions. It is dominant (alone or in combination with another aspect) in 13 out of 31 cases. The involvement aspect slipped into 26 (out of 40) Howard and Sheth descriptions, most often in a complementary way. In eight (always three-dimensional) cases it even dominates the description, in two of them in combination with the effort aspect.

Distinguishing between 'entangled' and 'not entangled' discussions further adds to the variety of Howard and Sheth descriptions. Astonishingly in 22 out of all relevant (namely, multidimensional) cases, entanglement is considered to be present, leaving only 16 non-entangled cases.

Table 4.3 Contents of the Howard and Sheth discussions (judges' consensus evaluation)

Source	Emphasis on			Entanglement	Other typologies
	Stage	Effort	Involvement		
Type 1 One-dimensional, stage interpretation					
Howard and Sheth (1969) formal definitions, p. 27	VS	No	No	N.a.	N.a.
Howard and Sheth (1969) formal definitions, p. 418	VS	No	No	N.a.	N.a.
Type 2 One-dimensional, effort interpretation					
Type 3 One-dimensional, involvement interpretation					
Type 4 Two-dimensional, stage dominated interpretation					
Zaltman and Wallendorf (1983)	VS	No	H	No	Involvement
Howard (1989) formal definition, pp. 364–91	VS	S/VS	No	No	N.a.
Howard and Sheth (1967)	VS	S/VS	No	Yes	No
Howard (1977)	VS	S/VS	No	Yes	No
Lunn (Sheth) (1974)	VS	S/VS	No	Yes	N.a.
Howard (1989)	VS	S	No	Yes	No
Bettman (1979)	VS	S	No	Yes	Involvement, variety seeking
Lawson (Baker) (1995)	VS	H	No	No	Boredom problem solving, involvement, impulse
Howard (1963)	VS	S	No	Yes	No
Howard and Sheth (1969)	VS	M/S	No	Yes	No
Type 5 Two-dimensional, effort dominated interpretation					
Type 6 Two-dimensional, involvement dominated interpretation					
Type 7 Two-dimensional, stage–effort dominated interpretation					
Schiffman and Kanuk (1994)	VS	VS	No	No	Involvement
Williams (1982)	VS	VS	No	Yes	Involvement, impulse, complex problem solving
Rewoldt, Scott and Warshaw (1981)	VS	VS	No	Yes	No
Type 8 Two-dimensional, effort–involvement dominated interpretation					
Type 9 Two-dimensional, stage–involvement dominated interpretation					
Type 10 Three-dimensional, effort dominated interpretation					
McCarthy and Perreault (1993)	VS	S	M/S	No	No

cont'd

Source	Emphasis on			Entanglement	Other typologies
	Stage	Effort	Involvement		
Lusch and Lusch (1987)	VS	M/S	M/S	No	No
Oliver (1986)	VS	S	H/M	Yes	No
Guiltinan and Paul (1994)	VS	S	M	Yes	No
McDaniel (1982)	VS	S/VS	H	Yes	No
Howard (1974)	VS	S	H/M	Yes	No
Horton (1984)	VS	M	H	No	No
Zikmund and d'Amico (1996)	VS	S	M	No	Involvement
Wilkie (1986)	VS	S	M/S	Yes	Involvement
Type 11 Three-dimensional, effort dominated interpretation					
Bearden, Ingram and La Forge (1995)	S/VS	VS	M/S	No	Involvement
Pride and Ferrel (1991)	S	VS	S	No	No
Dibb et al. (1994)	M/S	VS	S	No	Impulse
Solomon (1994)	M/S	VS	M/S	Yes	Involvement
Peter and Olson (1994)	M	VS	S	No	
Hawkins, Best and Coney (1992)	H/M	S/VS	H/M	No	No
Engel, Blackwell and Miniard (1986)	H	VS	S	No	No
Type 12 Three-dimensional, involvement dominated interpretation					
Kinnear and Bernhardt (1986)	S	S/VS	VS	No	No
Doyle (1994)	S/VS	S	VS	Yes	Impulse/ sensual/ image
Tarpey, Donnelly and Peter (1979)	M	S/VS	VS	Yes	No
Runyon (1977)	H/M	S/VS	VS	Yes	Impulse/ brand loyalty
Markin (1982)	H	M	VS	Yes	No
Bovée, Houston and Thill (1995)	H/M	S	VS	Yes	No
Type 13 Three-dimensional, stage–effort dominated interpretation					
Cravens, Hills and Woodruff (1980)	S	S	H	Yes	No
Type 14 Three-dimensional, effort–involvement dominated interpretation					
Brassington and Pettitt (1997)	H/M	VS	VS	No	Impulse
Jobber (1995)	M	S/VS	S/VS	No	Involvement
Type 15 Three-dimensional, effort–involvement dominated interpretation					
Type 16 Three-dimensional, stage–effort–involvement dominated interpretation					

Notes: VS = very strongly; S = strongly; M = moderately; H = hardly; N.a. = not available.

A remarkable finding is also that even within a given text, different parts of a description sometimes bear a different accent. An example is Pride and Ferrell (1991, pp. 140–1), who provide RRB and EPS descriptions that are equally involvement- and effort-dominated, the stage element being rather secondary. Their LPS description, though, is a pure stage definition as postulated by Howard and Sheth, with similar effort implications. Besides inconsistencies within the text, schematic representations sometimes carry a different accent in comparison with written text parts. McCarthy and Perreault's description (1993, pp. 219–20), for instance, is hardly entangled, but their graphical representation (p. 219) is.

Findings from the study: the popularity and presentation of the Howard and Sheth typology

More than half of the 127 sampled textbooks (67) do not contain any buyer behaviour typology. Of the 60 textbooks including a buyer behaviour classification, those containing the Howard and Sheth typology (37) by far outnumber those not containing it (23). If textbooks written or edited by Howard and/or Sheth are left out, this observation still holds: 31 versus 23 textbooks refer to the Howard and Sheth taxonomy. *This makes Howard and Sheth by far the most popular buyer behaviour taxonomy, followed by involvement typologies.*

Another striking observation is that authors formally present the Howard and Sheth typology in a fairly personal manner. The labels of the typology show some variation. Solomon (1994, pp. 218–19), for instance, uses terms such as Routine Response Behaviour and Habitual Decision Making instead of Routinised Response Behaviour. In some textbooks, the original Howard and Sheth framework is represented in a slightly different but still recognizable way. Pride and Ferrell (1983, pp. 72–3), for example, picture and define 'Routine Decision Making' and 'Extensive Decision Making' as extremes between which a continuum is postulated, without, however, naming LPS. In other texts, though, the source of inspiration supposedly must have been Howard and Sheth, but their framework is hardly recognizable. Schoell and Guiltinan (1995, p. 132), for instance, locate buying situations on a continuum, the extremes of which are almost synonyms for Howard and Sheth terms. At one extreme they place Complex Decision Making (an Assael 1985/1992 term, defined by Schoell and Guiltinan as extensive problem-solving) and at the other Programmed Decisions (defined as routine decisions). Some textbooks more recognizably fit the Howard and Sheth terms into a broader classificatory framework. An example is Doyle (1994, p. 248), who cites a typology based on involvement and rationality. The high rationality half of his classification distinguishes between EPS, LPS and RRB, and relates these terms to decreasing involvement levels. Other textbooks fit consumer behaviour types different from Howard and Sheth's into the Howard and Sheth framework. Brassington and Pettitt (1997, p. 96), for instance, discuss impulse purchasing as a major subcategory of Routine Problem Solving.

Generally, the link with original Howard and Sheth publications is weak. It is particularly noteworthy that not one single source uses literal quotations to define Howard and Sheth concepts. In more than half of the relevant cases, no reference is made to Howard and Sheth, or very exceptionally an Howard and Sheth source is taken up in a literature list without any specific mention in the text. Some of these textbooks present the typology as 'generally accepted', using expressions such as 'buying decisions are typically categorised' (Guiltinan and Paul, 1994, p. 67) or, 'Consumer decisions are often described as' (Bearden, Ingram and La Forge, 1995, p. 111). Another astonishing aspect, even when happening only exceptionally, is that reference is made to a source other than Howard and Sheth (e.g., Guiltinan and Paul, 1994 refer to Wilkie, 1990).

Last but not least, textbooks seldom derive implications or recommendations from the Howard and Sheth typology. Only one out of four cases derive direct and explicit guidelines in terms of marketing strategy and/or instruments. In cases where conclusions are drawn, this is most often done rather concisely and unsystematically.

Negative outcomes from the study

Content analysis reveals remarkable biases in the discussions of the Howard and Sheth stage classification. Even though the typology is clearly a popular one, *many textbooks reproducing it distort its contents, without any formal comparison with the original sources*. This section investigates possible reasons underlying these findings, and points to the negative consequences.

Misleading labels

The diffusion process of the Howard and Sheth concepts has presumably been influenced by the specific choice of the labels. One may wonder whether the terms EPS, LPS and RRB completely suit the category definitions and intentions of the authors. The linguistic distinction between Extended and Limited Problem Solving refers to a difference in magnitude of problem-solving rather than to a sequence of stages (see, e.g., Hornby, 1989, pp. 425 and 724). So, based on common understanding in everyday language and without direct help from a formal source, EPS is spontaneously associated with elaborate and complex situations, and LPS with smaller and less difficult problems. The RRB label, and in particular the expression 'Response Behaviour', linguistically evokes isolated, automatic and instant reactions Hornby (1989, p. 1,077). As a result, the label tends to narrow down this type of decision-making to situations with a high purchase frequency. Yet RRB is intended to be a general stage concept, applicable to all types of good, irrespective of the frequency with which they are bought. It should also be mentioned that some variation occurs in the use of the labels by the original authors. In 1963 Howard used the term 'Automatic Response Behaviour', which in the 1967 publication (together with Sheth) became 'Routinised Response Behaviour' until he replaced it in 1989 by 'Routine Problem Solving'. All three labels, however, have a connotation of instantaneous and repetitive reactions.

Minor textual inaccuracies by Howard and Sheth

There is no doubt in our opinion about the fact that Howard and Sheth intended their typology to be stage-based. This does not mean, though, that no differences in explanation occur within and between their own publications. Indeed, some minor differences in choice of words and emphasis do occur. These may have confused or unintentionally misled other marketing authors.

Factual dominance of some buying situations in reality

The previous inaccuracies partly explain the prominence of the effort dimension in Howard and Sheth textbook discussions. They do not, however, explain the presence of three dimensions instead of just one, or the high entanglement of these dimensions. A major reason underlying the entangled nature of most discussions may be the factual dominance of some buying situations in reality. Pragmatic grouping of the most common buying processes observed in practice would probably lead to a description of three types: (i) routine purchases for low involvement products involving little effort, (ii) comparative buying situations with moderate effort for moderately important products, and (iii) purchases characterized by much effort to acquire high involvement products that are seldom bought.

Consequences of the distorted transfer of the Howard and Sheth typology

The Howard and Sheth descriptions encountered in most textbook fragments produce an oversimplified picture of consumer buying behaviour, mainly as a result of their entanglement. These overgeneralizations are neither correct nor in line with Howard and Sheth publications. In reality, stage and effort do not always coincide. In some instances, EPS hardly requires any problem-solving, whereas the LPS stage may absorb much energy. Similarly, stage and importance do not always coincide. Even though people are more likely to develop automatic choice processes for less important and frequently purchased products, very important items may enter into a habitual purchasing stage too. Finally, effort and importance need not coincide. Relatively important products are sometimes bought after a very concise decision process – an example being the purchase of a new car after a major car accident – and vice versa. Also, the nature of two buying situations demanding a similar amount of cognitive effort may differ markedly. Not entangled Howard and Sheth discussions do, in principle, leave room for less likely situations such as quick purchases of important products, yet most of these not entangled discussions do not at all describe or analyse these less likely cases, although they exist and are important. Most textbooks therefore fail to recognize the full complexity of the buying process. Not only are readers not informed about less common situations, but often the suggestion is made that these situations do not exist. In neglecting these less straightforward buying situations, marketing textbooks fail to deal adequately with the reality of consumer buying behaviour. This implies a major opportunity cost. It prevents the transfer of more advanced and newly developed knowledge, which does not fit into the simplified presentation, to a wider audience. It also inhibits the use of such knowledge in the many differentiated and also evolving buying situations encountered in reality, each calling for appropriate managerial action.

Positive outcomes from the study

The Howard and Sheth typology can be considered as the prime consumer behaviour classification of the discipline. Over the years, however, it seems to have started a life of its own, no longer firmly connected with its original authors who developed it, but this phenomenon may also have some positive consequences.

Projection context

The absence of formal definitions and references may, to some extent, provide a 'cue' to the Howard and Sheth terms. It is as if the presentation of these terms to textbook authors not only makes them summarize what they retained from more formal, earlier study, but also makes them add various associations. In other words, the descriptions authors provide partly become projections of their logical and empirical associations with the three Howard and Sheth labels. It is as if many authors have unknowingly contributed to a 'Think Tank' of marketing specialists aiming at putting forward the major dimensions for classifying consumer-buying situations. As a result, the sum of viewpoints and considerations found under the Howard and Sheth headings is far larger, more diverse and richer than the original descriptions. Although some of the output of this 'Think Tank' is a bit crude, the major dimensions around which thoughts have evolved are quite clear. Basically, they relate to the amount of search effort, learning through time and the importance of the product category in that order. These three aspects or dimensions could be disentangled to better represent the differentiation and richness of buyer behaviour found in reality. They could be named and scaled properly. In combination, these dimensions could lead to a comprehensive buying behaviour framework sustained by the experience and insight of many textbook authors. As a result of its origin and nature such a scheme – described in the next section – could well be called the 'Think Tank typology'.

The Think Tank typology

The stage aspect of the buying process – as pictured by Howard and Sheth – constitutes a first basic dimension to distinguish between buying situations. However, as the Howard and Sheth labels suggest intensity of search activity or effort rather than stages, it would be better to adopt a different set of headings to denote the stage categories. The terms 'concept formation', 'concept attainment' and 'concept utilization' are suitable candidates. These terms gained status in psychology, show little ambiguity and would not be mixed up with effort and involvement categories.

A second dimension of the Think Tank typology would be search effort. The division of the effort dimension into three categories seems to be a straightforward and practical arrangement in the eyes of many. Many marketing authors indeed use the Howard and Sheth terms following this interpretation. They use terms such as 'extensive' and 'extended' to indicate relatively high levels of effort, and terms such as 'limited' or sometimes 'virtually none' for moderate and low levels respectively.

The notion of product importance, brought up by many authors when discussing the Howard and Sheth labels, would be the third dimension of the Think Tank typology. It corresponds with the concept of involvement, and especially with enduring involvement with the product category. As in many textbook discussions and similar to the other dimensions, a trichotomous split seems most appropriate: more specifically, a distinction between low, moderate, and high involvement buyer behaviour.

To obtain an idea of the comprehensiveness of this Think Tank typology, the authors tested to what extent this (3×3) scheme is capable of catching different published types of consumer behaviour. In particular, they tried to fit the full set of behavioural types encountered in their literature study into the Think Tank framework. It is found that all these types can easily be captured by the Think Tank typology. It follows that this (3×3) typology represents an extremely comprehensive framework. Based on the sampled evidence, it even possesses the property of collective exhaustiveness. Given these appealing features, one may wonder whether the Think Tank typology could not serve as a generic buyer behaviour typology.

A critical 21st-century managerial perspective

Against the earlier list of desirable properties, our content analysis suggests that textbooks tend to perform rather poorly from the point of view of practitioners. Even though not all textbooks are alike, our study uncovers a pattern of problems that seems to prevent many of these books adequately fulfilling their role *vis-à-vis* practitioners. Exceptions not withstanding, 'typical' textbook discussions score rather poorly on most of the criteria a 'typical' manager supposedly would use for typology descriptions.

The classic Howard and Sheth typology bears rather ambiguous labels. In view of the fact that professional (textbook) authors seem to be carried away by those labels, there is little doubt that the average reader risks being misled by them. The ambiguity of the labels may have been a (valid) reason for some authors to introduce labels of their own, explaining some of the heterogeneity of labels encountered across textbooks. Yet, while Howard and Sheth themselves used slightly differing definitions within and across their publications, textbook authors' definitions differ to such an extent that it is virtually impossible to find two completely identical descriptions. For managerial readers, this hardly provides solid ground for developing a clear understanding of the Howard and Sheth typology or, for that matter, of other typologies. Moreover, exceptions notwithstanding, average textbooks do not offer a very clear, explicit treatment of the specific, relevant behavioural aspects of the Howard and Sheth concepts.

Our content analysis further reveals that differences from other buyer behaviour typologies are seldom discussed. The same goes for combinations. A manager who would, for instance, be interested to learn about the specifics of impulse buying of durables in their RRB stage typically remains uninformed. Equally, typical textbooks say hardly anything concerning new scientific findings that would shed new light on the Howard and Sheth concepts. The implications, for instance, of the more recent high/low-involvement distinction for the classic Howard and Sheth concepts are not available in typical textbooks.

Finally, most textbooks fail to provide an in-depth discussion of the tactical and strategic implications of the Howard and Sheth types, either in an isolated fashion or in comparison to other types. The typical textbook says very little, for instance, about the timing of communication efforts, communication media and messages for brands within an EPS context.

The implications of textbook deficiencies for practitioners mainly come in the form of opportunity costs. For instance, managers could have spent their time and money more usefully than on possibly superficial textbooks. Much more important, though, are the opportunity costs from less well-prepared, postponed or cancelled decisions, because of the lack of reliable textbook guidance. Apart from their personal and business opportunity costs, practitioners might also wonder about opportunity costs of all the public and private money going into the academic sector.

In the face of this reality, individual reactions of practitioners may differ widely. The less brilliant and/or more docile ones will hardly notice any deficiencies as they may only access one book (i.e., the current 'best seller'). In contrast, brighter and more demanding types of practitioner may arrive at a rather negative verdict. On the one hand, they may decide to fall back on their own analytical, intuitive and judgemental capabilities.

Alternatively, they may turn to other sources deemed more relevant (but also more costly) than textbooks, such as business or marketing consultants who are always circling overhead, or the permanent hiring of employees who presumably understand and can deal with plurality and ambiguity in conceptualization and 'see the individual trees in the wood', rather than 'the wood in the trees'.

A critical 21st-century academic perspective

Given that academics are those writing most of the marketing textbooks for dissemination it is presumed that adequate knowledge transfer through marketing textbooks is a major prerequisite for sensible generation and use of marketing knowledge. The Howard and Sheth typology appears as an exemplar of deficient knowledge transfer. Even though it is normal – and probably unavoidable – to encounter minor differences in the descriptions of basic concepts and typologies by different authors, the variations observed in the Howard and Sheth case are well beyond any such minor differences. Discrepancies in 20th-century textbooks are overwhelming, and jeopardize an adequate absorption of information on essential aspects of the typology. Given that the Howard and Sheth classification is probably one of the most frequently used and often-quoted basic building blocks of marketing in textbooks, to structure one of the major subfields, it is difficult to believe that the problems observed in the Howard and Sheth case are in fact isolated examples.

We hypothesize that these are indicative of a more widespread 20th-century phenomenon in the marketing discipline. We conjecture that in marketing textbooks up to the moment of this appraisal, basic building blocks have generally been transferred too loosely. Lack of formal referencing and quoting are one aspect of this. Absence of minute study and comparison of the contents of basic concepts is another. Perhaps the drive to 'publish or perish' is a major determinant of these factors? For textbook authors in marketing seem to deal with basic building blocks in a rather approximate, intuitive and creative way, starting from accepted jargon. But the jargon serves too much as a mere cue, not as the terminological counterpart of a solid set of concepts and classifications. The meaning and use of terms therefore becomes unduly elastic.

The Howard and Sheth study also leads to the conjecture that marketing textbook authors complement basic concepts and classifications with ad hoc, improvised comments rather than with systematic consideration and research findings that relate to strategic and tactical applicability.

Under these conditions, the output of scientific production does not and cannot possibly go much further than the ivory tower in which it is produced. Only a tiny fraction of applied and scientific research results are actually conveyed to ultimate users, which represents a tremendous opportunity cost for the marketing discipline.

From a 21st-century perspective, disciplined information transfer is a strict prerequisite for further integration of existing knowledge, which, in turn, is the necessary fertile soil to foster the development of new insights. Absence of integration leads to inefficiencies (scholars inventing the wheel again) and entails difficulties in the comparison and interpretation of empirical findings, the derivation of behavioural laws, and the formulation of managerial recommendations. Given these high stakes, the marketing discipline should more actively pursue integration of related terms, concepts and typologies, and look for wider and more all-embracing typologies. Such integration requires thoughtful pooling of existing information. It implies careful analysis and comparison of isolated elements, using explicit criteria. Good review or state-of-the-art papers do exactly that, and should be more actively solicited by prominent journals and conference organizers. Encouraging ad hoc committees or other occasional Think Tanks to review and summarize the status of subfields of the discipline is another fruitful option. Integration should be followed by consolidation. This means that accumulated knowledge should be registered in a 'lasting' form (even when made available electronically), and should be widely accessible. An example would be lists of definitions constructed by representative bodies such as the Chartered Institute of Marketing or the American Marketing Association. This does not mean that no upgrading should take place; on the contrary, continuous development of ideas is of crucial importance, but this should be done in an explicit, argued and verifiable way, starting from a clear body of already accumulated knowledge.

Integration and consolidation clarify the current state of the art and, in doing so, set the stage for further development. They may even lead to the conception of truly generic classifications. This is also illustrated by the Howard and Sheth case. The integration of fragmented textbook information leads to the development of the Think Tank typology, which may have the potential to become a generic buying behaviour classification. Incorporating these types of conceptual frameworks in marketing textbooks ensures that these textbooks indeed serve as dependable and reliable conveyers of marketing knowledge, and do not risk acting as gatekeepers, inhibitors or bottlenecks in the transfer of such knowledge. Truly generic classifications foster the emergence of more advanced and new findings, and enable greater relevance to ultimate users of marketing knowledge.

The previous discussion can lead to no other conclusion than that the issue of imperfect knowledge transfer through marketing textbooks is important. Too much time, effort and money – in the form of opportunity costs – are involved to neglect the issue at the beginning of the 21st century. In the new century, strong mechanisms are needed to consolidate existing scientific work, and to make it available to users in an appropriate fashion. Incentives are needed for researchers to elaborate on the practical consequences of their research, and to convey their insights to practitioners instead of just to scholars (Winer, 2000, for example, argues a similar case from the context of marketing modelling). Possible instruments to pursue this could be a compulsory section on practical implications in academic journals, or reliable rating systems of textbooks by sector organizations. Certainly, there is a real need to involve practitioners to a far greater extent in the pursuit of marketing knowledge, and to provide academics with the incentives not to multiply textbooks without accompanying deep thoughtful analysis of how particular conceptualizations can be decoded and operationalized.

Professionalism in marketing: an oxymoron?

5

michael thomas

Introduction

Neil Ascherson (Ascherson, 1999), in an essay on Tom Paine, wrote that 'the sightless psychopath of market forces' had become sovereign; that 'all that could be or should be done was to worship him, the only sin was to obstruct his reeling onrush'. He was writing about the political climate of the first Thatcher administration. The following question is posed in this chapter: are we, professional marketers, 'the sightless psychopaths of market forces'? The aim of this chapter is to examine the nature of professionalism, particularly what we will call civic professionalism. We will contrast it with market professionalism, the name we give to current perceptions of the practice of marketing. We will ask what may have to develop if marketers are to become social trustees, trusteeship being the hallmark of a civic profession.

Epistemopathology: marketing sickness

We will argue that the marketing profession, most particularly in its academic trappings, suffers from 'Epistemopathology'. Epistemopathology is diseased, sick and bad knowledge that is mechanistically applied to contemporary (global) market systems, in self-serving ways, to identify and solve immediate problems which are not well understood and without any consideration of the ripple effects on society as a whole. Lindbloom (1990) calls this tendency 'impairment'. Senge (1994) refers to it as 'organisational learning disability'.

We live in a global world, a world fashioned by the machine, the factory, the assembly line, and which is supported by increasingly sophisticated information systems operating in and through networked large-scale bureaucratic organizations. We are trained and educated in industrialized, bureaucratized schools, colleges and universities. The profession of marketing is an instrument of a market-driven, industrialized, bureaucratic society. We are steeped, indeed brainwashed, in mechanical, market-driven professionalism. Our watchwords are planning, organizing, motivating, controlling, stability, conformity, predictability, regulation. The post-modernists are threatening that world. Ambiguity, complexity and chaos threaten our cosy self-defined world. Future shock and paradigm shifts are in post-reality, the world we now inhabit.

Six critical questions

In this chapter, we are going to concentrate on citizen professionals. As members of the marketing class (perhaps we are Chartered Marketers, or marketers that consider ourselves qualified in some way) we should be anxious to know what a claim to professional status in marketing entails. In a wider context, we are interested in the role of the professions in our society:

1   Do citizen-professionals really demonstrate social responsibility?

2   If consumer freedom of choice epitomizes the dichotomy between the citizen professional and the private citizen, can interdependency be re-established?

3   Can democracy, citizenship and socially responsible professionalism be made the hallmarks of the 21st century?

4   Today, mechanical, market-driven professionalism prevails and social trusteeship has been compromised: is this epistemopathology or organizational learning disability?

5   Can we invent social trusteeship in our profession? Can mutual empowerment and constituent practice theory help?

6   How can citizen professionals be educated? Can they contribute to the transformation of the sightless psychopath?

Implicit in the questions is a contrast between what can be called mechanical, market-driven professionalism and social trustee, civic professionalism. This chapter will dwell on these two constructs, since it is the author's contention that the marketing profession must re-define itself in its social trustee role if it is to survive. We do not wish to imply that all marketing professionals are capable of performing only in the mechanical mode. We do contend, however, that awareness of the social trustee role is much too low, too ill-defined and amorphous, and that, in the training and education of marketing managers, the subject is totally neglected. The great challenge for educators and practitioners in the 21st century is to address the destructive elements of market-driven capitalism, to build the bridges necessary to relink the citizen professional and the private citizen. The profession of marketing should clearly demonstrate that its practitioners subscribe to a set of moral values. Social morality is about balancing short-term gain against possible long-term detriment. Today we appear to live in a climate where short-termism rules our actions. It is a disease of market-driven capitalism and, if the issues are not addressed, the very fabric of the system may implode.

First a set of statements relating macro-forces and factors to the development of mechanical, market-driven professionalism. I am grateful to Dr Hal Lawson, formerly of the University of Utah, now at the State University of New York, Albany, for this list (Lawson, 1998):

1 Steady development of the philosophies and world views associated with the Enlightenment, especially growing secularization of social life worlds as science and scientific reasoning is increasingly substituted for religion and traditional values.

2 The ideology of progress associated with technology, one of science's stepchildren.

3 Rapid industrialization facilitated by technology in concert with the development of market economies, a dynamic interaction supported by some religious doctrine and utopian worldviews such as Progressivism.

4 Continuing transition from communal organization and cohesion (*Gemeinschaft*) to utilitarian, exchange-minded, individualistic forms of association (*Geselleschaft*).

5 The accommodation and development of liberal democratic theory and its institutional expression, the welfare capitalist state.

6 Devaluing of traditional values, which has accompanied the rise of relativism, utilitarianism and positivist determinism; and, in turn, constructed dichotomies between theory and practice, the individual and the state, and public and private knowledge and spheres of action.

7 The growing domination of two root metaphors – machine (and assembly line) and organism (and disease) – in approaches to

problem-setting and problem-solving, together with growing optimism that people and institutions in society and all things in nature are subject to human intervention, regulation, change and control.

8   The concomitant rise and democratization of universities and, in turn, the ideas of the scientific expert and systems of experts (professions).

9   The mutual accommodation of the universities and emergent professions, and later, their academic disciplines, reflecting and fuelling a political (market) economy of professions in the community and 'parent' disciplines in universities.

10   Commitment to social engineering and management technologies performed by experts in administrative–legal bureaucracies and the transformation of psychology to serve these ends and promote the growth of the discipline.

11   Blurring of distinctions between private goods and public goods as production–consumption patterns escalated.

Those who may be interested in pursuing the historical background to these statements should consult Perkin (1996).

Two types of profession

In Table 5.1 an ideal–typical contrast has been constructed, which compares mechanical market-driven professionalism with social trustee civic professionalism. For convenience and comprehension this table is divided into six segments: purpose and orientation, work and action orientation, root metaphors and systems, narration and orientation, theory–practice framework, and competition versus co-operation. Within each section, marketers (practitioners and academics) may be able to position themselves so as to obtain a clear distinction between the two typologies. However, the entire table can be seen as an aide-memoire to the key concepts and ideas espoused in the chapter.

Based on Table 5.1 a series of thought-provoking questions can be asked:

1   What is the current relationship between purpose and orientation in the marketing profession? Does this need radical change? (See Table 5.1a.)

2   What needs to be done to change attitudes towards work and behaviour? How does this impact on the marketing profession? (See Table 5.1b.)

Table 5.1 An ideal–typical contrast between mechanical, market-driven professionalism and social trustee, civic professionalism

	Mechanical, market-driven professionalism	Social trustee, civic professionalism
(a) *Purpose and orientation*		
Primary purpose	Improvements in one aspect of human development and performance, namely buyer–seller relationships.	Holistic improvements in better human beings; citizenship in a good society.
Identity orientation	Split: work as applied scientist is separated from personal life.	Integrated: life and work are unified in scholarship of practice-as-praxis.
Knowledge orientation	Rational individualism and method-determinations.	Relational social actions and language-determinations.
Power orientation	Top-down: professional knows best.	Shared: people served have expertise and knowledge.
Names for persons being served	Client, consumer, customer.	Citizen, child, youth, parent, family expert.
View of persons being served	Needs, problems, deficits.	Aspirations, needs, wants, and strengths.
Attribution framework	Personal troubles: needs, problems, deficits exist in individuals because of their orientations and actions; market-led solutions address the problems of needs and wants.	Social issues involving causes such as poverty, unemployment, family stress, racism, sexism, ethnocentrism, class, homophobia, and blocked aspirations are weighed along with individuals' responsibilities.

Critical commentary: these contrasts are meant to stimulate thinking about the differences between market oriented attitudes and behaviours and those associated with civic professionalism. The definitions are tentative as yet, but begin to provide a basis for differentiation of attitude. Note in particular that market driven professionalism is predominantly short term in orientation (offering quick-fix mechanistic solutions), whereas civic professionalism is holistic and addresses long-term problems with responsible human beings at all levels taking part in developing solutions.

(b) *Work and action orientation*		
Orientation towards persons being served	Professional distance and emotional detachment.	Empathy, advocacy, caring and strategic supports.

cont'd

	Mechanical, market-driven professionalism	Social trustee, civic professionalism
Focus of work	Individuals' behaviour and characteristics, sometimes in groups formed by professionals and organizations.	Individuals, groups and families in concert with their home–community environments; social and natural environments.
Work organization	Bureaucracy.	Learning organizations.
Criteria for good wok	Units of service delivered, fidelity to rules and norms specified by supervisors and the organization.	Improvements in shared learning, developing goals, social trust and quality of treatment.
Action orientation	Fidelity in technology application and programme implementation.	Co-construction and evaluation of warranted, collaborative, generative practice and change theories.
Work orientation	Method-bound, role-taker; tendency to fit the person to the method(s) and programme(s).	Role-maker: personalized and tailored service; responsive to person, cultures, and contexts.
Focus and primary beneficiary of the work organization	Clients, consumers, students.	Professionals and persons served because their well-being is interdependent.

Critical commentary: the contrast between bureaucracy and learning organizations, the method-bound role-taker versus the role-maker, is fundamental to understanding the contrast between market-driven professionalism and civic professionalism. The question must be asked as to whether the currently fashionable customer relationship marketing/management (CRM) is really addressing the challenge implicit in the description of the role-maker.

(c) *Root metaphors and systems*

Organizational directions	Administration and management: following proper procedure so things are done right.	Leadership: ensuring good results because the right things are done, at the right time, for the right reasons.
Career orientation	Individualistic: mobility and prestige stem from personal achievements.	Collective as well as individual: mutual responsibility for stewarding each other and the people served.

cont'd

	Mechanical, market-driven professionalism	Social trustee, civic professionalism
Table 5.1 cont'd		
Root metaphors	Machine (assembly line), organism (disease).	Social ecology, drama (play, stories).
Reference	Reductionistic, specialized, and categorical.	Ecological, relational and interdependent.
System	Specialized, monopolized language of intervention, compliance, adherence, reinforcement, control, and regulation with reference to descriptive–explanatory 'mechanisms'.	Democratized language expressed and shared through empowerment-oriented social pedagogies: social trust, mutual aid and assistance, norms of reciprocity, identity development, meaning making, social responsibility with reference to citizenship, well-being, and the good, just society.

Critical commentary: in this segment, implications for marketing educators are clear. The right product, the right price, the right place, at the right time are supplanted by ensuring good results as a result of the right things getting done, at the right time, for the right reasons. The contrast between the two systems provides a very sharp distinction between control and empowerment-oriented pedagogies.

(d) Narration and orientation

Style of narration	Passive voice: the facts and the world speak for themselves and values, ethics, morals do not belong because they are private and subjective.	Active voice: the facts and the language that expresses them are human inventions told through, and understood as, value-referenced stories (narratives).
Cultural orientation	Assimilation referencing social capital theory; cultural diversity poses problems and needs for control.	Mutual accommodation referencing social–cultural capital theory; cultural diversity is an asset.
Kind of rationality	Formal: methods (means) and goals are determined by weighing alternatives; means may become ends and may cause harm.	Substantive: democratized socio-rational practices ensure that human and societal welfare are served.
Theory of change	Simplistic: usually restricted to psychological micro-theories for professionals' selected	Complex: micro-, meso-, and macro theories are identified, harmonized and synchronized

cont'd

	Mechanical, market-driven professionalism	Social trustee, civic professionalism
	socio-psychological programme theories.	to generate mutually-beneficial synergy; the boundaries between science and social–moral issues in democracies are maintained.
Temporal–spatial orientation	Often ahistorical and place insensitive: statistically-determined generalizability, and objectivity-as-quantifiable data dominate.	Time- and place-sensitive with social priorities assigned to memories and traditions in relation to future needs and goals: generalizability is a substantive concept weighed against ecological validity.

Critical commentary: the 'Think Global, Act Local' issue can be applied to both columns with interesting results. Diversity and complexity, time–place sensitivity and ecological validity are questions to be addressed seriously by civic professionals, in contrast to the ahistoric and place insensitive approaches of market professionals.

(e) *Theory–practice framework*

Philosophical grounding	Positivism and post-positivism.	Neo-pragmatism; classical social science, which integrates philosophy, history, sociology and psychology; aspects of post-modernism.
Imagery of knowledge use	Behavioural and social engineering.	Participatory-democratic planning and decision-making.
Theoretical orientation	Cybernetics and systems theory, chaos theory.	Social ecological theory, developmental contextualist theory.
Knowledge production dynamics	Knowledge results from trained scientists in controlled laboratories or laboratory-like settings: research produces knowledge.	Knowledge also results from reflective and reflexive practices of professionals and the people they serve: academically-based community scholarship yields knowledge while doing good work.
Theory–practice frame	Theory is constituted by facts and propositions gained through empirical observations; theory is value-free; practice is the rule-governed behaviour of individuals.	Theory begins with value-referents regarding good, just, sustainable societies; empirical observations help map and monitor pathways towards the realization of these visions;

cont'd

Table 5.1 cont'd	
Mechanical, market-driven professionalism	Social trustee, civic professionalism
	practice is an exercise in the social construction of theories in pursuit of these visions (praxis).

Critical commentary: positivism and post-positivism versus post-modernism may characterize this section. Can marketing professionals grasp the implications for them of the emphases shown in the second column? Can they grasp why it is necessary to define the nature of good, just and sustainable societies prior to defining marketing best practice?

(f) Competition versus co-operation

Legitimization strategy	Conventional: keeping up with the Joneses who are perceived to be prestigious and successful.	Confidence that the future will provide a more rational and fairer society for all.
Orientation towards civil society	Indifferent, perhaps ignorant; market focus.	Committed stewardship and nurturing of play, freedom.
Ethical–moral grounding	Codes of ethics and claims to service are impression management devices designed to protect professional jurisdictions.	Codes of ethics and social–moral practice norms are emphasized in preparation programmes and evaluated in practice.
Discipline–professional relationship	Often conflicting and disconnected: mission drift and epistemic drift are commonplace.	Symbiotic and harmonious: requirements for socially–responsible work and collective accountability criteria and structures for it are prioritized and honoured.
Relationships with other helping fields	Competitive: individuals, groups, and entire fields claim jurisdictions and compete for markets, cultural power and authority; children, adults, and families are caught in the middle and may be harmed.	Collaborative: inter-professional education and training programmes supported by community partnerships prepare professionals to work together and share accountability for interdependent outcomes.

Critical commentary: current thinking about marketing is embodied in the first column. Fundamental challenges to these current ways of thinking about the marketing professional are embodied in the second column.

3 What root/core metaphors and systems characterize the marketing profession? Is significant reconsideration necessary? (See Table 5.1c.)

4 Should human and societal welfare needs be served? What role does marketing play in this? How does this impact narrations and orientation? (See Table 5.1d.)

5 How does marketing theory impact upon current marketing practice? (See also the chapter by Walter van Waterschoot and Els Gilbrecht.) What theoretical constructs need to change or be amended? How will this impact future marketing practice? (See Table 5.1e.)

6 Should attitudes towards competition be supplanted by more co-operative approaches? How does this impact on current perceptions of customers and consumers? How does it impact organizational structure and competitive structure? (See Table 5.1f.)

Now let us turn to a second, but inter-related issue that also impacts significantly in the drive toward more civic-minded professionalism: the ongoing (and perhaps irresistible) drive towards globalization.

The impact of globalization

Globalization is the phrase used to describe growing global interdependence, a process that Theodore Levitt (1983) described as homogenizing the people, practices and nations of the world. The process has been aided and abetted by accelerating advances in communications and information technologies, and worldwide systems of finance, monetary exchange and trade. Homogenization is not necessarily welcomed by all, since it challenges peoples' identities, meanings systems, cultural values and forms of social organization. Interdependency is threatened by the collapse of economic systems (Argentina and, perhaps, Japan), environmental degradation, the spread of AIDS, increasing income inequality, economic migration, and most obviously, since 11 September 2001, international terrorism.

We want to propose that, in the era of globalization, social trustee civic professionalism must rule. Narrow self-interest must no longer characterize our professionalism. Citizen professionals must minister to the needs and wants of other citizens. We must not pretend, as we have, that we regard the needs and wants of consumers as the grist for our mill, for the needs and wants of some customers cannot be equated with the needs and wants of our citizens.

We envision paradise as a globally networked society, dedicated to promoting social welfare, with citizen professionals dedicated to sustainable, integrated, equitable, social and economic development. Citizen professionals will promote democracy and ensure social responsibility. In other words, instead of being self-serving, method-bound, narrowly focused profession members, we will become social trustees of the common good. We will have a clear, comprehensive vision of the good and just society and its place in the world order. We will abandon our pretences about value-neutrality and objectivity (our inheritance from the philosophy of science) and focus on ethical–moral, social responsibility as it confronts the citizens of global, cosmopolitan democracies. We are prepared to be accused of utopian thinking (Carey, 1999).

Social trustee civic professionalism

Figure 5.1 provides a model for understanding civic professionalism in its social trustee dimension. This model may help us to explore a new approach to the role of marketing in civil society.

We marketers have in some respects become the victims of our own success. If we differentiate between the marketing concept and the function of marketing, there is evidence that senior management in most British and American companies have at last absorbed the concept, though it has taken several decades. Companies have understood that they must be market-driven, and hence everyone in the company (or organization) must be market-driven. Thus ownership of the ideological resource known as marketing knowledge now extends beyond our specialism and threatens to dissolve its distinctiveness and its identity. We believe that too much of the myth and not enough of the codified knowledge is being claimed by non-marketing specialists. We believe that corporate management, though claiming to understand the marketing concept, still confuses trappings with substance. We would cite four examples:

1   Accountants will rarely admit that the marketing function is the primary revenue generator and cash flow provider to the company. If firms do not market their products or services effectively and efficiently, wealth does not flow back into the organization to underwrite costs already incurred, and profit streams are unlikely.

2   The Operations Function tends to be pre-occupied with production (the Japanese have taught us all why production must be focused on the marketplace and marketplace acceptance). Such a focus, however, has already receded into the past sedimentary strata of marketing history.

3   Research and Development frequently hold marketing in low esteem despite strong evidence that the reason most new products fail is due to a lack of adoption by the target market.

4   We find very few Human Resource executives who understand why a company's telephone operators are part of the marketing team.

The problem is one of integration, and of driving substance, *not trappings*, through every organizational level, so the firm or business is customer-focused, which implies change for every organizational structure and for every employee within that structure. Most firms have not taken this required step towards marketing, nor indeed considered subsequent steps taken after that first stage.

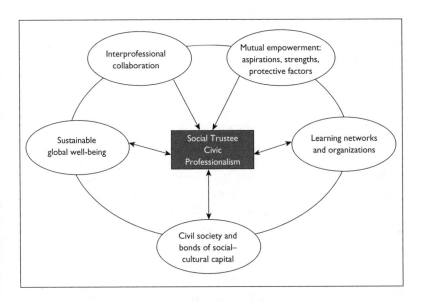

Figure 5.1   Mutual determinants of social trustee, civic professionalism

Comment: this figure (after Lawson, 1998) attempts to summarize the crucial and cardinal points of the preceding table regarding civic professionalism. Further explication requires reference back to the table. The inter-linkages are crucial. The development of civic professionalism will impact upon global well-being, on inter-professional collaboration, on empowerment, on learning networks and organization, and on the bonds of social–cultural capital. Without real civic professionalism, epistemopathology will impair all elements of the total system.

The challenge facing the profession of marketing

Thus, the challenge facing our profession is to demonstrate, both within corporations and at the highest political levels, that we are not only masters of our information-based technology, but that the precise skills of marketing, namely planning, logistics and creativity, based on superior understanding of the global marketplace, of market forces, and the need to deliver superior value, are the crucial determinants of future corporate survival and success; they are necessary, but not sufficient, conditions.

Now, what is it that we need to do to become more professional?

1   We need to come to terms with finance, we need to be able to argue effectively with the accountancy profession, to persuade them profit is not merely the bottom line, but the residual effect of successful dealing with customers and society in general, and that most marketing activities are an investment, not a cost.

2   We need to demonstrate that we are the professional experts in respect of marketing information, and as a consequence we must come to terms with information technology (IT), since we are the people best equipped to exploit the facilities that IT capability provides.

3   We need to rethink our attitudes towards brands and brand management: 'Brands now cause trouble, not because they dictate tastes, but because they allow companies to dodge civic obligations ... Brands will be trusted to serve as cultural source materials when their sponsors have demonstrated that they shoulder civic responsibilities as would a community pillar' (Holt, 2002).

4   We must play an active role in driving Total Quality Management (TQM), since TQM can only work in a customer-driven culture if it is clearly understood that the customer's assessment of value added is frequently co-terminous with quality.

5   We must think strategically, from the top, and recognize that in the future companies will be constructed according to customers (or perhaps customers' customers), and not to product, geography, or function as has traditionally been the case. The marketing silo should be dismantled, but our professional skills will be in demand at the top of the organization and at all interfaces with the customer.

Marketers will not become more professional until they address these issues. Our critics argue that markets are organized for purposes of exploitation not fulfilment, that marketing as a function does not possess a monopoly of understanding human wants and values, that and '*mar-keting's rapacious orientation to consumer needs is more plausibly attributed to the dynamics of capitalism than it is to the development and application of marketing expertise*' (McKenna, 1991).

The most powerful criticism is presently directed at the changed role of global corporations. 'Corporations are much more than the purveyors of the products we all want, they are also the most powerful political forces of our time, the driving forces behind bodies such as the World Trade Organisation' (Klein, 2000). Global corporations appear to operate above the law, in the sense that the law operates at the level of the nation-state, and global corporations can escape responsibility – to pay tax, for example – by moving operations from one national jurisdiction to another. There is as yet no Geneva Convention for global corporations. Additionally, we may note the power exercised by global corporations over national policies. America's rejection of the Kyoto Agreement was surely done at the behest of American corporations rather than because of some more highly-principled objection to its objectives.

As a profession, we have an unparalleled opportunity. We must demonstrate by our professionalism that we are crucial to the survival both of the organizations we claim to serve and to society in general.

The rhetoric of marketing

Marketing does have a powerful rhetoric. It is not lacking in ideological materials. It is much more than a set of techniques for the management of external markets. Our flexible ideology, our disposition to accept change as the inevitable consequence of the interplay of market forces will (unless we are careful), however, be hijacked by others, for quite different purposes.

We must improve our reputation as a knowledge generator, through strategic linkages and alliances with leading-edge knowledge generators. We must demonstrate, perhaps by benchmarking, that the most successful companies are those that are truly market-driven and responsive global citizens.

We, as marketing professionals, and as marketing educators, must be developing insights that pre-empt the future.

More urgently perhaps, we must recognize that in addition to high standards of objectivity, integrity and technical competence, we must, in responding to the changing environment, demonstrate that we can and will serve society in general. This requires clear and articulate demonstration of our ability to be relevant in the political sense. Accountants have been successful in part because they have been so obviously servants of Anglo–American capitalism with its historical focus on finance, though the Enron debacle may prove to be their undoing. Though this is not the correct forum to discuss this, we could develop an argument that this historic focus has served us poorly in competition with the Japanese. In the global economy, and in the face of the competitive forces within it, it is the company and the country that delivers value to the marketplace and to society that will survive. If we remain tied to the forces of manipulation and hype, if we are seen merely to be the servants of our capitalist masters, we will remain marginal and untrustworthy. Thus, we have to demonstrate the enhanced value associated with marketing. And, in our move to greater civic-minded professionalism, we have the keys to the knowledge base that will benefit society as a whole. If we turn those keys effectively, then we as marketers and our profession may prosper.

Conclusion: the critical questions revisited

To conclude we return to the six questions posed at the beginning of this chapter:

1   Do citizen professionals really demonstrate social responsibility? We have argued that our current view of the marketing profession is far too narrow. We anticipate that the forces of globalization will demand that our view of our obligations will require more focus on the welfare of society and community – local, regional, national and global, rather than on customers.

2   If customer freedom of choice epitomizes the dichotomy between citizen professional and the private citizen, can interdependency be re-established? That is the challenge that faces us all, and for which there is no easy or glib response. The re-orientation of the marketing profession will require radical rethinking about measures of success. Stakeholder value rather than shareholder return will be the first goal. Questions must remain as to whether market capitalism can effectively embrace such radical thinking.

3   Can democracy, citizenship and socially responsible professionalism be made the hallmarks of the 21st century? This is the fundamental challenge facing our century. If global terrorism is energized not just by religious values but by the resentment nurtured by vast inequality in living standards, then the very future of democracy is at stake.

4   Today, mechanical, market-driven professionalism prevails and social trusteeship has been compromised. Epistemopathology or organizational learning disability? The sources of our present orientation and the possibilities for re-orientation require us to examine the whole basis of our approach to education and training.

5   Can we invent social trusteeship in our profession? Can mutual empowerment and constituent practice theory help? We believe that there is a theoretical base that can be used to assist us in our thinking about transformation.

6   How do you educate citizen professionals? Can they contribute to the transformation of the sightless psychopath? This is the challenge facing marketing educators!

We hope that this chapter will contribute to the debate as to how we educate citizen professionals.

Note that there are no easy answers to the questions raised. We do believe that the current marketing curriculum is far too narrow, almost entirely wedded to the mechanistic viewpoint. Education is a very serious business, and the retailing of today's fashions in marketing techniques is *not*, emphatically *not*, the purpose of education. The logic of our position suggests that undergraduate marketing education be dropped, to be replaced at the very least by a curriculum oriented towards politics, philosophy and economics: five parts philosophy to one part each of politics and economics! Marketing may need to become a post-graduate and/or post-experience subject. Realistically, such reform would be of little consequence if our masters, in the centres of power and influence in national governments, in Brussels, in the United Nations, and most particularly in Washington, fail to realize the consequences of short-termism. Fed by the greed of narrowly-focused, remuneration-fixated senior executives, supported by manipulative accountants, given no clear understanding of the consequences of the rich–poor divide in both national and supra-national environments by the political leadership of the most powerful nations, the global economy is rushing headlong into the zone where implosion is a real possibility. The 'evil empire', global terrorism, global warming, the African AIDS epidemic and the Enron affair are all symptoms of the wider epistemopathology. That is why the debate about civic professionalism needs to be entered into with urgency (Thomas, 1996; 2002).

How clients can improve their advertising by improving their decision-making

john philip jones[*]

Introduction

Manufacturers and service organizations have to make marketing decisions of two types in managing their advertising: financial ones and creative ones. Financial decisions – those regarding advertising budgets – are made at a high level in corporate hierarchies, and by the most experienced executives. This is because expenditures are often large. Creative decisions – those concerning actual content of campaigns – are made at a much lower level and are often rubber-stamped by executives at the top. From any perspective, this is a deeply flawed system, as we shall see, because the financial and creative decisions are intimately related. Without effective campaigns, financial investments are wasted. In addition, a substantive proportion of campaigns are in fact either weak or totally ineffective, as measured by reliable data. In relation to a critical 21st-century perspective on marketing, this chapter considers several crucial questions pertaining to a major component of marketing, and one in which substantial resource allocations are made.

[*] I am grateful to Simon Broadbent, formerly of Leo Burnett, and Jeremy Bullmore of WPP, for valuable comments on earlier versions of this chapter, which itself is an expanded version of an article 'Advertising: The Cinderella of Business', *Market Leader*, 9 (2000), published by the World Advertising Research Center and used here with permission.

1   Does advertising expenditure really matter to most firms?

2   How is advertising managed?

3   What is the trade-off between profit and advertising?

4   Does or should advertising have an immediate effect on consumer purchasing?

5   Why should advertisers ever run ineffective advertising campaigns?

The chapter is concluded by offering four types of radical action, *needed now*, in order to produce more effective advertising that impacts on the bottom line. The implications of these suggestions are spelled out in terms of a critical 21st-century perspective on marketing.

Advertising expenditures really matter to most firms

How do senior managers spend their time? Opinions vary. At one extreme we have the view of the cynic, that business leaders allocate their time and energy to tasks in inverse proportion to task importance. At the other extreme, we have the utopian view that leaders are guided by a vision and devote all their efforts to its long-term realization, and of course there are all the variations in between.

The way I have looked at senior managers in large business organizations has been from the specialist perspective of an advertising practitioner working with and observing major clients. From my view of the field, over a period of more than 40 years, leaders as seen by the cynic represent no more than an insignificant minority, but managers of the utopian type are not the dominant majority that they ought to be.

My specific orientation and observation has led me to note one significant feature of all types of executives, good and bad: not one spends *any serious* amount of time on the advertising operations of their companies, and certainly none on the qualitative content of their campaigns. I am not referring here to corporate/public relations campaigns which many senior executives run like a hobby, and to which they devote inordinate attention despite such campaigns' often peripheral value. Neither am I thinking about businesses in the fashion and cosmetic fields, whose advertising is often evaluated with flair by the heads of such businesses, who have often built their reputation by being creative themselves. No, these are the exceptions and not the rule.

My argument focuses on brand advertising, a subject of ever-increasing importance, in the main line consumer goods categories; advertising that is – or should be – the daily bread and butter of the companies operating in these categories.

The neglect of such advertising by senior executives has always seemed surprising, bearing in mind the actual size of the marketing investments involved. During the period 1995–2000, all advertising expenditures in the USA were on a modestly upward push, although the internal composition of the aggregates remained stable. In 1998, a typical year, each of the ten largest advertisers in the United States spent $1,764 million on average (nearly $2 billion), made up of $1,090 million on measured media (i.e., advertising on television, newspapers, radio, magazines and billboards), plus $674 million on unmeasured media (i.e., direct mail, specialist journals, the Internet, etc.). A further 120 firms each spent more than $200 million, and another 74 spent over $100 million. In other words, a great deal of financial resources are being allocated or invested in the promotional medium.

Senior executives are alone responsible for making the financial decisions regarding advertising for the obvious reason that the sums are large and impact significantly on corporate profitability. However, in view of the size of such investments, it is puzzling that senior managers seem to be so little concerned with *how* this money is deployed. Even more strangely, why are they so distressingly uninterested in ensuring reliable accountability to find out whether these sums yield a profitable return? It is not an exaggeration to suggest that advertising has become, or is becoming, the Cinderella of business; it is certainly not a Cinderella in investment terms. Why, then, the apparent lack of attention to accountability and measurability? To answer this question, we need to explore how advertising is managed.

How advertising is managed

I believe that the most important reason why advertising receives so little close attention at the top level of firms is an organizational one. Because advertising has for long been regarded as a subjective, artistic and 'unbusinesslike' activity, most advertisers that spend substantial amounts on it develop rather rigid internal systems for handling it in a 'businesslike' way, starting with evaluating the proposals that are submitted by their advertising agencies. Many large advertisers have rules (sometimes explicit and sometimes tacit) that must be followed in the execution of their advertising. For convenience I shall use the phrase Company Advertising Policies (CAPs) to describe these.

In many cases these policies are underpinned by the mandatory use of special types of market research, in particular pre-testing techniques to examine commercials before they are run. The trouble is that such research is used blindly: as a pointer to whether the advertising should be used or not. Not much attention is paid to *what* the research is actually showing; in many cases the findings are far removed from indicating a commercial's selling power. Inefficient evaluation of creative ideas carries the direct cost of sales sacrificed by the inadequate advertising that it screens in, plus the opportunity cost of lost sales from potentially effective advertising that it screens out. Such systems need careful observation, which means comparing research findings and subsequent marketplace performance of the advertisements tested. Not only do many advertisers fail to do this, but most are unable to do it even if they wanted to!

Let me describe the CAPs of two real but disguised companies: Agamemnon Inc. and Oedipus Inc. These are both massive multinational organizations selling fast-moving consumer goods (fmcg), and are also in direct competition.

Agamemnon Inc. For more than 20 years, Agamemnon's CAPs were so restrictive that they permitted only one type of creative execution for the advertising of its multitude of variegated brands. This style of advertising stemmed from the company's belief in a single type of pre-testing research: a method based on recall of the advertising and not on its selling power. After two decades of using it and the expenditure of many billions of advertising dollars, the company found this research to be non-predictive (i.e., it was essentially useless). The abandonment of this system, together with the creative straitjacket it imposed on the company's advertising, led to a relaxation of the CAPs, although even now they still remain uncomfortably rigid.

Oedipus Inc. Oedipus's CAPs date from the early 1960s. Each element within the company's book of rules has a title, and the whole procedure is described with an acronym familiar to everyone in the company engaged in advertising operations. The characteristics of what the company considers to be effective advertising are embodied in another familiar acronym. The whole system is taught to brand managers through training programmes conducted worldwide.

Within these two firms – and in countless others – advertising proposals regarding campaign content are discussed first at a low level in a company's hierarchy: by brand managers who are the initial (and main) point of contact with advertising agencies. Proposals at this stage are naturally judged in terms of how well they adhere to previously understood CAPs.

When proposals are accepted by brand managers, they are sent up the chain of command (sometimes through six different levels), and often accompanied by succinct documents (ideally only a page in length) providing reasoned support and summarized research evidence (some of it highly questionable) that said proposals follow the spirit and the letter of the CAPs. When the proposals reach the level of management at which substantial sums of money have to be approved, senior executives who must spend the money will be more concerned with reviewing the reasoning of their subordinates than evaluating the advertising proposals *per se*. It becomes more a matter of routine supervision (i.e., giving the thumbs up or down to the recommendations of subordinates). What perhaps started life as a motivational factor – for brand managers and potentially customers or consumers – in creative and investment terms has become a hygiene factor at senior organizational levels (i.e., the maintenance of a norm).

Whatever the reasons – because advertising is considered too unimportant, or too low on the company's pecking order, or too incompatible with the culture of senior executives – the greatest judgemental engagement with the company's advertising takes place *at the lowest levels of a company's managerial hierarchy*. The job is done by the least experienced managers. They can, as indicated, select things that they will pass to higher levels; this is the extent to which they are empowered to say 'yes'. On the other hand, they can reject things on their own initiative: they can say 'no' without reference to their superiors. Since they are not very experienced and their judgement is still being developed, this process can lead to many babies being thrown out with the bathwater.

There is also a further problem stemming from advertising agencies. These organizations are too often regarded by their clients as mere suppliers. Very few agencies today have any serious research capability. And during recent years, the media function has been hived off to separate organizations, which means that even large agencies have all too frequently become creative boutiques.

Agencies very rarely carry out a regular dialogue with the senior executives of their clients' companies, beyond quasi-social contacts. The early pioneers of the advertising agency business, men such as Albert Lasker and Stanley Resor, were considered by the most senior of their clients to be genuine partners in business. And the generation of agency leaders who dominated the business after the Second World War – William Bernbach, Leo Burnett, Marion Harper, David Ogilvy and Rosser Reeves – had the personality and the authority to command respect from the highest levels of their clients' organizations. One of the most striking features of advertising during the past 30 years has been its loss of cachet. The reasons for this loss are complex, but I am certain that it has contributed substantially to the low level of interest in advertising felt by senior executives of large firms.

The trade-off between profit and advertising

It is common practice for a manufacturer's advertising budget to be compared with its sales value in order to calculate its advertising-to-sales ratio. (This ratio for the ten largest advertisers in the United States is 1:25, but the share varies from advertiser to advertiser.) The importance of this piece of simple mathematics is that it helps us to compare, without too much finesse, the relative importance of advertising to businesses of different types and sizes.

However, a significantly greater and certainly more useful analysis can be made by another simple calculation: *a comparison of a manufacturer's advertising budget with its earnings*. There is a good reason for this.

In running a business, direct (variable) and indirect (fixed) costs have first claim on the business's receipts. The remaining calls on its revenue – advertising, sales promotions, and distributed and undistributed profit – are paid out of the residual. It therefore makes sense to look at the trade-off between each of these residual items. More advertising means less money for sales promotions and profits; less advertising means more money for sales promotions and profits.

This chapter is not concerned with the trade-off between advertising and sales promotions, although I have examined this in another context and concluded that from most points of view advertising is a vastly more valuable tool for building business in the long term, since sales promotions generally have no prolonged effect at all, besides biting to an unacceptable degree into a brand's profit.

My examination of advertising and sales promotions was first published in the *Harvard Business Review* in 1990 and subsequently republished in a number of other places. The thrust of my argument was that the response of a brand's sales to a price reduction (i.e., a promotion) is always greater than the response to an advertising expenditure increase, but that the cost to the manufacturer of the price reduction is always far greater than the advertising boost. This means that the large volume increases stimulated by promotions are hardly ever profitable, but smaller increases driven by advertising often are. In addition, as indicated, advertising can have an additional long-term effect which is something denied to promotions.

Although this is an interesting and (I believe) important matter, I cannot develop it further here. My concern in this chapter is the comparison

Table 6.1	Leading US advertisers: net income compared with advertising expenditure	
	US net income/ operating profit ($ million)	US advertising measured plus unmeasured media ($ million)
General Motors	1,228	2,940
Procter & Gamble	2,710	2,650
Philip Morris	5,134 (gross)	2,049
Daimler/Chrysler	2,800 (estimated)	1,647
Ford Motor	6,685	1,521
AT&T	6,398	1,428
Sears, Roebuck	1,984	1,578
Walt Disney	3,468	1,359
Pepsi	1,629	1,263
Diageo	1,535	1,206

Source: Adapted from data that appeared in the 27 September 1999 issue of *Advertising Age.* Copyright Crain Communications Inc. (1999).

between advertising and profit as a contribution to a critical perspective of marketing in the 21st century. This comparison is illustrated in Table 6.1, which is (again) based on 1998 data.

The average earnings of each of the ten advertisers in Table 6.1 were $3.4 billion. The average advertising expenditure was $1.8 billion. The advertising figure is sufficiently close to earnings for there to be a significant trade-off between the two expenditures. Based on the above averages, a 20 per cent decrease in advertising would boost earnings by more than 10 per cent, assuming that the advertising reduction left sales unaffected (an assumption we shall shortly examine).

This analysis is *not* leading to a general recommendation to reduce advertising in order to increase profit, no matter how directly proportional the trade-off between the two amounts may be. Cutting advertising expenditure can be extremely dangerous to brand health unless the advertiser has ironclad evidence that the campaign is having no effect.

The urgent reasons for the comparison between advertising expenditure and profit are that:

(i)   it emphasizes the importance of determining a brand's optimal advertising budget (a very difficult procedure, although advertisers and agencies should not give up trying to do it); and

(ii) *it should cause alarm bells to ring if robust evidence shows any advertising to be failing.*

How do we provide reliable evidence of the effectiveness or ineffectiveness of specific campaigns? Let us look at what we know about the general patterns of response of consumer purchasing to advertising. This is a matter about which we have learned a great deal during the past decade.

Advertising's immediate effect on consumer purchasing

The source of the data described here is a simple but expensive research technique called Pure Single-Source. The findings of this research have been widely disseminated throughout the advertising world.

This research has revealed facts about advertising effectiveness which were either unknown or known to only a few analysts by instinct or from fragmentary evidence. Here are four conclusions – all based on behavioural data (i.e., measures of purchasing rather than on measures of cognitive or attitudinal change) – which I believe are now accepted fairly widely:

1   Advertising is capable *on its own* of producing short-term, medium-term and long-term effects on consumer purchases of a brand. Short term means within one to seven days of an advertisement's exposure. Medium term means across the course of a year. Long term means beyond a year and far into the future.

2   Advertising does not always – or even very often – produce all these effects.

3   A short-term effect is a pre-condition for medium-term and long-term effects. Advertising does not work as a sleeper or like a time bomb. The short term is therefore critically important as a gatekeeper to longer-term effects. This gives the lie to the lingering belief that even if we can see no pay-off from advertising today, it will yield returns after more money has been spent on it. This is a myth of dangerous proportions.

4   The main influence on advertising's ability to generate a short-term effect is the quality of the creative idea within the advertisement. It follows that *the creative idea is the gatekeeper*. If this has no immediate effect, the gate must be closed and the advertiser has no alternative but to find a more effective idea. The budget will otherwise be wasted.

My conclusions were derived from large samples of American consumers and based on a detailed examination of advertising exposure and consumer purchasing of 78 fmcg brands. The basic data came from A.C. Nielsen, and very great care was taken to exclude the effect of stimuli other than the advertising that might affect sales.

The Nielsen system of Single-Source research was specially set up during the early 1990s and was based on Nielsen's ongoing Household Panel, a properly drawn sample of 40,000 households across the USA, in which every purchase of regularly bought brands is logged with hand-held scanners. In each home, the shopper uses the scanner to read the Universal Product Code (UPC) on each pack bought and thus records details of brand name, variety, and pack size. The shopper also punches in manually the date, the price, simple details of any promotional offers, the name of the store, and the identity of the individual doing the shopping. The information that has been fed into the scanner is sent to Nielsen by a simple automatic process over public telephone lines. The data gathering is continuous, or longitudinal, to use the technical language of statistics. The scanner system represents data collection of a highly sophisticated type. Nevertheless, it accounted for only one of three pieces of information needed for Pure Single-Source research.

The second process of data collection covered television viewing. This initial Nielsen study concentrated on television alone, although later studies by other research organizations also covered magazines. Nielsen selected a representative subset of 2,000 homes from its Household Panel and attached a meter to every television set in each home to record when it was switched on and to which channel. The viewing of individual family members was not recorded, but 'People Meters' enabled this to be done for the A.C. Nielsen Single-Source research in Germany, which was carried out after the American system was set up.

The third piece of research tackled the immense diversity of television viewing patterns: the large number of different channels viewed in each of 150 cities and regions in the USA. Nielsen used a system called Monitor Plus, which employs a series of television receiving stations that identify and log all the advertising that appears, at 15-second intervals, in the 23 largest Designated Market Areas (DMAs) in the United States, covering more than half the total population. Information is collected from all the main stations, both network and cable, in these areas.

There were thus three different streams of information: household purchasing, television viewing, and the identities of the advertised brands. I decided on a 'window' of seven days as the period during which a short-term advertising effect is assumed to be felt. Because the date when the brand was purchased was collected in the scanner, it became possible – with some difficulty – to identify whether advertising for that same brand had or had *not* entered the household during the preceding seven days. Nielsen took immense pains to devise the computer programs to generate the information that I specified (i.e., the difference in purchasing between the households that had received advertising for the brand, and purchasing in those that had not).

The basic idea behind the research was the concept of 'ad households' and 'adless households', as illustrated in Figure 6.1. A subtle but important characteristic of these two collections of households is that the groups were different *for every single purchase occasion*. With each purchase of any brand, the 2,000 households on the panel formed themselves into unique combinations of ad households and adless households, plus a third group who had not purchased the brand at all at this time. For the next purchase of a brand, the groups were mixed totally differently.

The tabulation of the data was extremely complicated, but this was a vital part of the process. We were examining constantly-changing combinations of the same collection of 2,000 households. The advantage of this system was that it guaranteed the homogeneity of the subsamples. The presence or absence of advertising was the sole variable distinguishing the subsamples on every occasion the brand was bought.

I employed a measure based on market share change, called Short-Term Advertising Strength (or STAS). Analysing these brands into deciles – groups representing 10 per cent of the total – the range of advertising effects follows the pattern shown in Figure 6.2.

Although, as indicated, the data came from various categories of packaged goods, there is no evidence of more uniformly positive effects from other types of advertising, with one single exception. This is direct

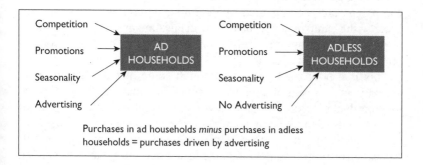

Figure 6.1   Ad households and adless households

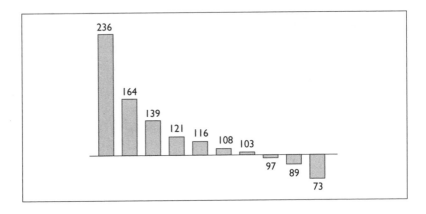

Figure 6.2   Range of short-term advertising strength effects

response advertising, which normally goes through meticulous testing via experimental exposure in one or two journals or one or two areas, before being used nationally. The result of taking such meticulous care is an eventual uniform level of effectiveness.

The data in Figure 6.2 are all indexed on a base of 100, so that the brands in the top decile show an average improvement in consumer purchases of 136 per cent. If readers are sceptical of the extreme (positive and negative) range of these effects, they should know that the research has been replicated with substantially similar results in the USA and in at least five other nations.

As can be seen from Figure 6.2, 30 per cent of campaigns produce a strongly positive short-term effect. Another 40 per cent of campaigns generate a positive but mostly small effect, and a further 30 per cent of campaigns are accompanied by declining purchases. (This happens because the campaigns for the brands in question are not strong enough to protect them from creatively stronger campaigns being run concurrently for competitive brands.)

This is a poor track record, although some business people may accept it as the result of a misconception. They may believe that, when total product categories do not show much overall growth, the gains of some brands (they hope their own) must be balanced by the losses of other brands (they hope other people's). This view ignores the possibility that advertised brands in the aggregate are quite capable of gaining market share at the expense of unadvertised brands (price brands and retailer labels), which account for more than one-third of all sales in many categories in the USA. I believe that a large amount of advertising should be expected to have a positive effect. The problem is that the advertising industry sets its sights too low.

I believe that the skewed and generally unsatisfactory short-term effectiveness of advertising is largely caused by *the small amount of attention that advertising receives in the upper echelons of client companies.*

Why should advertisers ever run ineffective advertising campaigns?

The range of advertising effects shown in Figure 6.2 should cause much unease to the senior managers of businesses which spend large advertising budgets.

It is facile, passive and possibly dangerous to respond to underperforming campaigns by cutting their budgets. It is far more important to improve – as a matter of great urgency – the creative content of failing advertising. This will turn an unproductive investment into a productive one. This is not a job for junior executives who work within a tight framework of rules; heavy guns must be employed. And what is needed is four types of radical action.

1   Measure behavioural effects

Serious money must be spent on measuring behavioural effects of advertising. Pure Single-Source Research is a *de luxe* solution for fmcg campaigns. But although this research can be set up at a price, it is rarely available as a standard syndicated service, although successful experiments have been carried out in Britain, Denmark, France, Germany and Norway to develop simpler but still reliable and practical systems.

Econometric work employing sophisticated mathematics is done by a relatively small number of the most successful advertisers in the USA. This is another *de luxe* system, which carries an above-average price tag. Such research enables an advertiser to deconstruct the annual sales of a brand in terms of its sources of business (i.e., to estimate how much volume has been derived from brand equity, television advertising, couponing, etc.). From this, it is possible to detect immediately the parts of the advertising and promotional (A&P) mix that are underperforming.

Surprisingly enough, high research costs can make economic sense. Hundreds of thousands of dollars can be spent productively on research if the advertiser has thereby saved ten times as much money by discontinuing an ineffective campaign. But taking this type of substantial financial decision based on judgement is a task for senior executives, not for brand managers.

Advertisers will obviously wish their campaigns to be in the group of the 30 per cent best performers, and they will also want to prolong these campaigns' effectiveness into the medium and long term. This has implications for budgetary and media policy, and we know a great deal about this. The findings of Pure Single-Source research have made an enormous impact on media strategy in the USA, where a strong move to Continuity Planning has taken place over the past five years. For many of the largest advertisers, this strategy is now being applied worldwide.

2   Do not stifle agency creativity

A short-term effect is determined (as explained) by the creative content of the advertising. Developing new campaign ideas to replace the duds requires talent, tenacity and stamina on the part of both the agency and the client. What the client can bring to the process is a calm and mature attitude of co-operation, allied to seasoned judgement. Again, these are not likely to be contributions that junior managers are able to make.

The load is very much on the shoulders of the advertising agency. For some years, clients have relentlessly been reducing agency remuneration per \$ million of billing. This has mainly taken the form of reducing rates of media commission, and it is difficult to see how this can be conducive to the unrelenting effort required to produce the highest quality of creative work, especially during a period of no overall growth in the business, as is happening now. Fees based on time-of-staff, plus agreed profit, are beginning to take over as the normal system of agency compensation, in the USA at least. But fees, like reduced rates of commission, must not be used as a means of starving the agencies. Agencies must be required to produce consistently (and, in such a competitive environment, increasingly) effective work, and they cannot do this without a comfortable enough income to attract the best talent.

3   Experiment and exercise quality control over advertising

Besides high-quality creative work, advertisers and agencies need to employ methods of exploring in a nurturing way the likely effects of advertisements in the marketplace. Many existing systems are inadequate and deserve the antagonism that advertising agencies feel towards much research of this type. But all too often some systems are used, and others rejected, on doctrinaire grounds. For example, prediction of a commercial's selling power based on a procedure that exposes an audience to an advertising stimulus (as part of an entertainment programme) and includes two lotteries to stimulate purchasing before and after the advertising, is a system with much to recommend it, on the basis of its impressive track record of accurate forecasting. But despite the hard evidence of its predictive power, it is rejected by many clients and most agencies for theoretical (and often also emotional) reasons. It is another major task for clients – again senior rather than junior management – to experiment with and exercise quality control over the whole process of evaluating and researching advertisements for their own brands.

4   Reconsider CAPs

All advertisers would also be well advised to reconsider the whole question of their Company Advertising Policies. The history of advertising has been littered with rules that have quickly degenerated into anachronisms. Advertisers should ask themselves whether they need rules at all.

Writing advertising (the agency's job) and evaluating it (the client's) are tasks that call for fresh unprejudiced minds that are capable of seeing unexpected inter-relationships. This is because the process of creating new ideas is essentially one of fusing connections – the most arresting ones being unexpected and unusual – between existing ideas. Although agency people tend to be more intuitive and clients more rational, both qualities are necessary. Good and effective clients have the highest regard for the special compound of sensitivity, originality and intellect that agencies can offer, and such clients realize that although agency people can be effectively controlled by a proper understanding of a brand's strategy (i.e., a set of objectives for the advertising), they work best if they are unfettered by restraints imposed on advertising *execution*.

Conclusion

This chapter has attempted to demonstrate that a good deal of current advertising performs inadequately in the marketplace, and this is quite frankly bad business. Locating any ineffective campaigns should be a matter of high priority for advertisers. Once these campaigns are identified, merely reducing or eliminating the budgets will improve profit but it will leave the brands dead in the water, and in increasing trouble. It is a far more fruitful endeavour to replace an unproductive campaign with a better one because this will in most circumstances cause sales and profits to grow.

The recommendations made in this chapter can only be implemented if senior executives are prepared to question and deliberately intervene in the way advertising is developed and approved at present within their organizations. Superior advertising cannot emerge from an essentially bureaucratic business environment; it can only be brought into being if top managers make the decision to transform and reinvigorate their companies' advertising efforts. This cannot happen until senior executives realize how important to their businesses advertising is, from both a qualitative and a quantitative point of view.

Clearly this chapter has implications for marketing communications in the 21st century. It is no longer sufficient to develop and evaluate advertising by using methods that may have been designed for previous stages of economic and social development. The 21st century will focus on brand communications from the context of a consumer-empowered society. One of the major (perhaps the major) contributors to brand sales, loyalty and equity is advertising. In the 21st century advertising is not just a delivery system, but also a retrieval and a meaning system. Increasingly, brand managers will use advertising alongside other promotional mix variables as part of an integrated marketing communications approach. Such an approach has resonance, not for tactical co-ordination of the promotional mix, but as part of refocusing communications on an outside-in approach to marketing *per se*. As advertising will play a significant role in message-meaning, so corporate executives, marketing managers and brand managers will have to reassess and reformulate ideas, concepts, structures and corporate advertising policies to match environmental forces. The arguments marshalled in this chapter are here to help facilitate the required adjustments.

Corporate branding: the marketing perspective

cees van riel and guido berens

Chapter aims

This chapter discusses the importance of corporate branding within the marketing field, and provides an overview of research on corporate brand associations (people's perceptions of corporate brands) and the influence that these associations may have on consumer behaviour. It shows that corporate brands and the associations people have with them play an exceptional role in consumers' judgements and decision-making processes.

Introduction and overview

During the last decades, corporate branding, or the management of corporate brands, has become increasingly important in the field of marketing. Corporate brands are names and logos that represent entire organizations rather than specific products, and therefore can be a symbol of the people, policies and values within an organization (Aaker, 1996). There are a number of reasons why corporate brands have become more important, some of which are closely related to the transformation of the whole field of marketing. In this chapter, we shall first discuss these reasons. Next, we provide an overview of research on the role that corporate brands play in consumer behaviour. Following on, we discuss the nature of the perceptions (associations) that people may have regarding corporate brands, and the role that these perceptions may play in determining their attitudes and behaviour regarding a company's products.

The importance of corporate branding

We stated that the increased importance of corporate branding is closely related to developments in the marketing field as a whole. So what are these developments? In the last decades, there have been important changes in the answers to two central marketing questions: (i) how customers and consumers make decisions regarding marketing exchanges, and (ii) how firms relate to their customers (Day and Montgomery, 1999). Regarding the first question, the ability of customers and consumers to gather information about what is available in the market has increased enormously because of the presence of the Internet. This development has made customers more demanding and has given them more power over companies. Regarding the second question, advances in information technology have made it possible even for large companies to keep track of the preferences of individual customers. As a result, many companies have begun to focus on the quality of the *relationships* they have with customers, rather than only the quality of the products they sell (Day and Montgomery, 1999; Leeflang, 2001).

Another, less recent, development is the increasing importance of services in most Western economies. In the marketing of services, the emphasis is naturally on the company and its relationships with its customers, rather than on tangible features (McDonald, De Chernatony and Harris, 2001). Even in the consumer product market, the rapid diffusion of new technologies has decreased differences between tangible product attributes, so that customers have to find other reasons for buying or not buying a certain product. The quality of the relationship that people have with the company that manufactures the products can be such a reason (Aaker, 1996). The increasing focus on relationship quality implies that the *organization* that delivers products and services is becoming more important in consumers' decision-making.

Apart from these developments in the field of marketing in general, corporate brands have become more important for other reasons. First, the increasing number of mergers and acquisitions in many industries forces companies to consider the *role* of their corporate brands in their brand portfolios. Thus they have to decide whether to profile themselves as one corporation using one corporate brand, as a parent company 'backing up' (endorsing) the subsidiary brands, or as multiple relatively independent entities using 'stand-alone' subsidiary brands (van Riel, 1995). In the first case, the corporate brand becomes the 'driver' (i.e., the reason why customers choose to patronize this particular organization). In the second case, the corporate brand serves as a general 'seal of approval', while a product brand provides the actual customer value proposition. Finally, in the third case, the corporate brand serves just to communicate with shareholders or the job market (Aaker, 1996).

Second, an increasing number of people demand companies to behave in a socially responsible way, and to provide openness about their operations. Naturally, openness to society is made easier when companies prominently show their corporate brands when communicating about individual products. From the perspective of the companies this can turn out to be beneficial or unhelpful. Thus, as is illustrated in Naomi Klein's (1999) well-known book, *No Logo*, companies such as Nike which use their corporate brands prominently in their product communications are especially vulnerable to public criticism. On the other hand, when such companies do stand the test of public scrutiny, as in the case of the Body Shop, they are likely to be held in higher esteem than companies that are less visible to the public, such as Procter & Gamble.

Third, the costs of developing and maintaining individual product brands (e.g., via advertising and commercials) has increased enormously in the last decades. For this reason, a lot of companies have relied on so-called *brand extensions* (i.e., the introduction of new products under existing brand names: see, e.g., Aaker and Keller, 1990). The rationale is that the new product benefits from the image of the existing brand name, so that minimal amounts of effort and money have to be spent in order to attract consumers to it. *Corporate brand extensions* are a specific case of brand extensions, in which new products are introduced under the corporate brand name (Keller and Aaker, 1998). Using corporate brand extensions would generally imply even larger economies of scale than 'ordinary' brand extensions. Such a strategy is, for example, pursued by Nestlé, a company that is increasingly positioning its products under the umbrella of one of its 'corporate' (worldwide) brands, such as Nestlé (Nescafé, Nesquick), Maggi, Buitoni and Perrier (see Parsons, 1996). However, as multiple studies have shown, a general prerequisite for the success of such extensions is that the new product fits reasonably well with the image of the original brand. When this is not the case, it may be that the new product not only derives little benefit from the existing brand, but even causes a dilution of the meaning of the original brand. Thus, there is a limit to which (corporate) brands can be 'stretched'.

Corporate brand associations

Corporate branding is thus concerned with the management of corporate brands. An important aspect of management of brands is to establish favourable associations that consumers and customers have with the brand. The question then is what kinds of associations people generally have with corporate brands, and how these associations differ from the associations people may have with product brands.

A number of classifications of corporate brand associations have been developed in the past. Mostly, this was done in the context of measuring corporate image or reputation among the public. In the late 1950s, the Opinion Research Corporation had already started doing large-scale surveys to measure corporate image. A factor analysis of some of these data showed a clustering of items according to the *social roles* that can be identified for a company, such as delivering quality products, being a good employer, supporting the community, and (we *are* talking about the 1950s) contributing to national defence (Cohen, 1963). Similar categorizations have later been used by *Fortune* magazine (since 1984) in its Most Admired Companies surveys (e.g., Sung and Tkaczyk, 2002), and recently by the Reputation Institute in its Reputation Quotient studies (Fombrun, Gardberg and Sever, 2000).

In our opinion, a useful classification is the one described by Brown and Dacin (1997). They divided corporate brand associations into those dealing with *corporate ability* and those dealing with *corporate social responsibility*. Corporate ability refers to 'the company's expertise in producing and delivering its outputs', corporate social responsibility to 'the organization's status and activities with respect to its perceived societal obligations' (Brown and Dacin, 1997, p. 68). Note that both types of attributes, strictly speaking, deal with responsibilities regarding society, since delivering quality products is also a responsibility. However, from the viewpoint of a consumer who is trying to evaluate a product, corporate ability is *directly relevant* to his/her evaluation, while corporate social responsibility is not. Thus, at least from a marketing perspective, it seems viable to make this distinction.

When looking at corporate websites, for example, one can frequently see a clear distinction between companies that focus mainly on their expertise in manufacturing good products, and companies that highlight their social conduct. Often, this seems to be determined to a large degree by the industry a company is in. Electronics companies, such as Sony or Bang & Olufsen, or companies that focus mainly on the business-to-business market, such as SAP, often mainly discuss their expertise and new products, whereas food or drug companies tend to put more emphasis on their social responsibilities. Additionally, there are substantial differences in the degree to which companies focus on different social responsibilities between different countries (Maignan and Ralston, in press). Within an industry there also can be large differences between the emphasis put on ability versus social responsibility. For example, in the pharmaceutical industry, Bayer mainly stresses its ability to develop innovative new drugs (see Figure 7.1), while Johnson & Johnson prominently displays its 'Credo', written by founder R.W. Johnson in 1943, concerning the company's obligations regarding a number of different stakeholders (Figure 7.2). While this document mentions the quality of products as the company's primary responsibility, it immediately makes clear that the company is dedicated to the interests of *all* its stakeholders.

What, then, makes such associations with corporate brands different from associations with product brands? One major difference is in the *content* of the associations. Thus, product brand associations only relate to product quality, while corporate brand associations also relate to other types of social role that the company as a whole has. However, it should be noted that 'product quality' also could include attributes that serve a role other than just enhancing the benefit of the customer, as for example in the case of environmentally friendly products. Likewise, for some corporate brands, people may only think of the overall quality of its products, rather than its other societal roles, and so the content of both types of association could overlap to some degree.

Figure 7.1   Bayer's positioning as an innovative, high-quality company

Source: www.bayerus.com (with permission)

Our Credo

We believe our first responsibility is to the doctors, nurses and patients,
to mothers and fathers and all others who use our products and services.
In meeting their needs everything we do must be of high quality.
We must constantly strive to reduce our costs
in order to maintain reasonable prices.
Customers' orders must be serviced promptly and accurately.
Our suppliers and distributors must have an opportunity
to make a fair profit.

We are responsible to our employees,
the men and women who work with us throughout the world.
Everyone must be considered as an individual.
We must respect their dignity and recognize their merit.
They must have a sense of security in their jobs.
Compensation must be fair and adequate,
and working conditions clean, orderly and safe.
We must be mindful of ways to help our employees fulfill
their family responsibilities.
Employees must feel free to make suggestions and complaints.
There must be equal opportunity for employment, development
and advancement for those qualified.
We must provide competent management,
and their actions must be just and ethical.

We are responsible to the communities in which we live and work
and to the world community as well.
We must be good citizens – support good works and charities
and bear our fair share of taxes.
We must encourage civic improvements and better health and education.
We must maintain in good order
the property we are privileged to use,
protecting the environment and natural resources.

Our final responsibility is to our stockholders.
Business must make a sound profit.
We must experiment with new ideas.
Research must be carried on, innovative programs developed
and mistakes paid for.
New equipment must be purchased, new facilities provided
and new products launched.
Reserves must be created to provide for adverse times.
When we operate according to these principles,
the stockholders should realize a fair return.

Johnson & Johnson

Figure 7.2   Johnson & Johnson's 'Credo'

Source: www.johnsonjohnson.com (with permission)

Another difference lies in the *sources* of the associations. Thus, while product brands and corporate brands may both be associated with product quality, product brands are generally narrow in scope, symbolizing one or a few products, whereas corporate brands often symbolize a whole range of products in different categories. Also, people may know whether a corporation invests a lot in research and development, has a lot of patents, or is able to attract the most talented employees. Such knowledge can lead to a more elaborate and confidently held impression than is obtained from knowledge about individual products. Similarly, while both types of brand may be associated with, say, environmental friendliness, for product brands this association is probably based on (marketing) communication regarding only one or a few specific products, whereas for corporate brands, environmental associations are more likely to be based on communication about the whole organization, including its people and policies (T.J. Brown, 1998). Thus, in general, corporate brand associations will be more *abstract* (i.e., based on more information) than product brand associations (Aaker, 1996; Maathuis, 1999).

Related to this, perceptions of a company as a whole generally also lead to an overall evaluation of the company in terms of its contributions to society (i.e., its *legitimacy*: see Handelman and Arnold, 1999). Such an evaluation is formed even when people are only familiar with the company's expertise in delivering products and services. In this case, a company may be evaluated based on whether its products and services advance the good of society. For example, when a firm has a poor track record in terms of quality, or produces a type of product that many people find harmful (such as weapons), its perceived legitimacy will tend to be low. Such evaluations are less likely to be formed for individual product brands, as they do not identify the company that can be held responsible.

When do corporate brand associations influence consumer behaviour?

We asserted above that one reason why corporate branding is important to marketing is that corporate brands and their associations are important to consumers and customers. But is this really true? That is, do corporate brand associations really influence consumer behaviour? Brown (1998), in an overview of the empirical literature on this subject, shows that this indeed seems to be the case. However, he makes two important qualifications. First, the influence of corporate brand associations depends on the *type* of association that is considered. For example, associations with corporate ability generally have a higher influence on perceptions of products, buying intentions and actual product buying behaviour than associations with corporate social responsibility (e.g., Cohen, 1963; Brown and Dacin, 1997).

Second, the influence of corporate brand associations can be strengthened or weakened by a number of conditions, so that it is not always present. Brown (1998) identifies several conditions, related to characteristics of the *consumers*, that evaluate the company's products, the *companies* themselves, and the *products*. Figure 7.3, adapted from his article, provides an overview of these conditions.

Characteristics of the *individuals* who evaluate the product determine whether they will recall many associations with the corporate brand when they encounter it and, if this is the case, whether they perceive those associations to be useful for evaluating the product. Thus, when consumers know little about the organization, the few associations that they have may have little influence on their product evaluations, because they do not come to mind easily when they see the organization's products. Conversely, when people know a lot about the organization, the

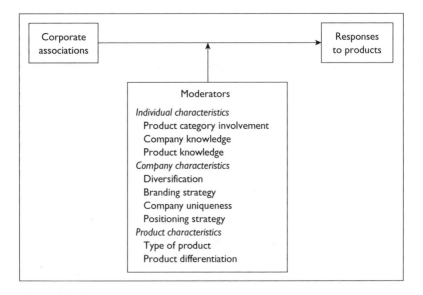

Figure 7.3 Conditions that can strengthen or weaken the influence of corporate brand associations

Source: Adapted from Brown (1998).

associations they have come more easily to mind, and therefore *potentially* have a larger influence on product evaluations.

When people know little about the type of *product* they are evaluating, they may find it useful to look at what they know about the company to provide some indication about product quality. Similarly, when people have a high involvement with the product (i.e., they find it personally relevant or enjoyable), they will probably look for additional sources of information when they want to evaluate it, including information about the company.

Attributes of the *company* itself may similarly determine the availability and usefulness of corporate brand associations. Thus, the *branding strategy* of the company (i.e., the prominence of the corporate brand in product communications) determines whether people actually think of the company when they are evaluating its products. Thus, when a company does not use its corporate brand when communicating about its products (as is the case for, say, Procter & Gamble), any associations that people may have with the company will not be particularly salient when they encounter its products.

When a company has an extremely diversified product portfolio (as does, for example, Unilever of Yamaha), perceptions of this portfolio may be less relevant for the evaluation of a specific product because they are too abstract to be very useful. For example, when consumers are looking for a very advanced piece of electronics, the fact that a company has a reputation for high quality in a number of different product categories may not give the assurance they are looking for. Consumers may only trust a company to deliver good quality in this respect when it has demonstrated expertise in just the type of product they are looking for. On the other hand, for less advanced products, a general 'seal of approval' from a reputable company may be very effective *because* the company has expertise in a number of different areas. In fact, a study by Dacin and Smith (1994) has shown just this. These authors demonstrated that the larger the number of products affiliated with a corporate brand, the more confidence consumers have in the brand, *provided* that the quality of the different products does not vary too much. Thus, although more products generally increase confidence, a specialized portfolio of consistent quality would still be better than a diversified portfolio of varying quality.

Similarly, when a company has a positioning that makes it unique among its competitors, people's perceptions of this company may be especially salient when they encounter its products, and therefore have a strong influence on their buying behaviour. By contrast, when a company is not unique, perceptions of that particular company may not be salient at all, and people may just think of it as 'just another...' (bank, supermarket, etc.). Of course, not only the uniqueness, but also the *content* of the company's positioning determines the degree to which corporate brand associations are perceived as useful. Thus, as stated above, a company's social responsibility is generally perceived as less relevant for the evaluation of the company's products than the company's ability. This could mean that companies that position themselves as socially responsible (such as the Body Shop) may be perceived very favourably by the public, but that this favourable perception may translate itself to a lesser degree in actual product sales than it does for companies who position themselves as experts in a certain area.

Finally, attributes of the type of *product* that is being evaluated also influence the relevance of corporate brand associations. Thus, when the quality of a product is hard to evaluate before purchasing (e.g., as in the case of food or complex services such as dentistry), information about the company that delivers the product may be useful to make a judgement. Similarly, when products in a certain category are very much alike (as, say, in hi-fi), information about the companies that produce them may provide reasons for choosing one brand above the other.

An empirical study

Some, but not all, of the above-mentioned propositions have been tested empirically. We therefore decided to conduct an empirical study that investigated a number of these propositions at the same time (Berens, van Riel and van Bruggen, 2002), where a large number of potential and actual customers of a financial services provider were interviewed regarding their perceptions of the company. For this, we used Fombrun, Gardberg and Sever's (2000) Reputation Quotient scale. The customers also evaluated a number of different products and services marketed by the company's subsidiaries (e.g., insurances, mortgages, investment services) shown on advertisements. These subsidiaries currently do not prominently show their relationship to the parent company (i.e., they are positioned as 'stand-alone' brands). To test the effects of different possible branding strategies, two versions of each advertisement were made: one with only the subsidiary brand (stand-alone), and one with a combination of the subsidiary brand and the corporate brand.

We found that perceptions of the company's ability (expertise) especially influenced the perceived quality of the products, whereas perceptions of the company's social responsibility (e.g., contributing to charity) especially influenced intentions to actually buy the products. Similarly, we found that corporate ability associations influenced product evaluations regardless of the branding strategy that was used. Consequently, even when the corporate brand was not shown on the advertisements, people's associations with the corporate brand's expertise had a positive influence on their product evaluations. In contrast, perceptions of the company's social responsibility *only* influenced product evaluations when the corporate brand was shown on the advertisements. This could mean that people use the ability of companies is used by people social to make an accurate judgement of a product's quality, whereas corporate social responsibility is used more to express one's values to others. This would explain why the latter type of perception would only influence product evaluations when the corporate brand is visible; when others cannot see who is the parent company behind the subsidiary one does business with, the parent company's social responsibility is not very useful for expressing one's values.

Our results also showed that the *involvement* that persons had with the products, and the *difficulty* they perceived in evaluating the product, determined whether their corporate brand associations influenced their product evaluations. However, it turned out that these determining effects were not independent of each other. Thus, corporate brand associations (especially regarding corporate ability) had a strong influence on product evaluations when people had a high involvement with the product *and* thought the product was difficult to evaluate. On the other hand, corporate brand associations also had a strong influence when people had a *low* involvement with the product and thought the product was relatively *easy* to evaluate. This implies that, in the first case, corporate brand associations serve as essential information which is used to make a better judgement of a product's quality, or to make a better informed decsision about whether or not to buy the product. In the second case, corporate brand associations are used as shortcuts or heuristics to save effort. The latter process can be thought of as a halo or context effect: people infer that a product marketed by the company must be good because they regard the company favourably on some other aspects, almost irrespective of whether those aspects are relevant for their product judgement.

In general, we can say that corporate brand associations, and especially corporate ability associations, influence product evaluations when people are not well *able* (but highly motivated) to make an accurate judgement of the product, or not very *motivated* (but well able), to make an accurate judgement. Thus, the results of our study provide some support for Brown's propositions, but they also suggest some qualifications.

Conclusion

Corporate brand associations have been of interest to marketers for over 40 years, but are currently becoming even more important. This is caused by developments such as the emphasis on relationships in marketing, the increasing importance of services in our Western economies, and the increasing amount of public scrutiny to which companies are subject. Empirical studies have shown time and again that consumers' perceptions of a company as a whole can have an important influence on their evaluations of the company's products, and thereby also on their purchase behaviour. However, it is also clear that this proposition requires some qualification. Thus, there are several types of perception that people may have of a certain company. For example, one can distinguish perceptions of a company's ability or expertise from perceptions of a company's social responsibility. These different types of association will tend to have different influences on product evaluations. As a result, the influence of different types of corporate brand association can be increased or decreased by different conditions related to the company, the product that is evaluated, and the person who evaluates the product.

In general, it can be stated that all corporate brand associations can serve a dual role in consumer behaviour. They either can be essential information that is used to make considered judgements and decisions regarding a product, or they can be used as convenient shortcuts when a person is not very motivated to make an accurate judgement. Corporate ability associations are primarily relevant for judging a product's *quality*. Associations related to a company's social responsibility, on the other hand, are more relevant for the *symbolic value* that buying a certain product may have, such as making visible a customer's commitment to certain good causes. These roles are roughly similar to the role of quality or 'life-style' perceptions regarding a product brand.

However, as discussed, there are differences. Perceptions of corporate brands, in contrast to perceptions of product brands, generally give customers an impression of the legitimacy of the organization, which may lead them to reward or punish companies for what they see as actions that advance or hinder the good of society as a whole. In addition, corporate brand associations are usually based on a lot of different information sources, creating a more abstract and well-founded impression than is generally formed regarding product brands.

Let's do the time warp again: a marketing manifesto for retro revolutionaries

8

stephen brown

Introduction and overview

A spectre is stalking marketing: the spectre of consumerism. All the powers of old marketing have entered into a holy alliance to exorcise this spectre: Kotler & Levitt, Grönroos & Gummesson, Procter & Gamble, Bang & Olufsen. But they are wasting their time. Consumers have had enough, more than enough. The anti-capitalist protests in Seattle and elsewhere; the boycotts of Nike and the Gap; the attacks on McDonald's and Starbucks; the best-selling status of ban-branding tracts such as *No Logo*; the egregious enormity of the Enron imbroglio; the dot.com meltdown that did for day-traders worldwide; and the rise of the Adbusting Angry Brigade, who expropriate marketing messages for hate-marketing ends, all attest to the power of the consumer counter-revolution (e.g., Cockburn, St Clair and Sekula, 2000; Frank, 2000; Klein, 2000; Monbiot, 2000; Bircham and Charlton, 2001; Bové and Dufour, 2001; Hertz, 2001).

Marketers too are getting in on the contra-marketing act. Apart from the recent rash of anti-advertising ads ('Image is Nothing', 'Fcuk advertising', etc.), which effectively expropriate the adbusting expropriators, the field has been beset by a closet-full of conceptual Cassandras, who 'out' themselves as life-long marketing sceptics, marketing doubters, marketing heretics, marketing agnostics or whatever. As the briefest browse in the business section of most mega-bookstores bears witness, anti-marketing polemics are two a penny. Management fadbusting is the latest management fad. The mockers have inherited the earth, or so it appears.

Step one: turn away

Clearly, it is impossible to paraphrase this multitude of marketing critiques, which range from Nigel Piercy's (2002) perennial protestations about the perfidy of marketing professors – himself excepted – to Locke's (2001) much-vaunted *Gonzo Marketing*, a shameless sales pitch for selling under the guise of not selling. As a rule, however, this critical marketing mass of mass marketing critics adopts a two-pronged rhetorical strategy: (i) mount an attack on old-style marketing; and (ii) propose a radical alternative, preferably one with a snappy title. For the purposes of the present discussion, these alternatives can be summarized (snappily, if I say so myself) under the following Eight Es:

1 *Experiential* – an emergent school of marketing thought that emphasizes ecstasy, emotion and the delivery of extraordinary consumer experiences (e.g., Schmitt, 1999). It exploits the 'Wow' factor, in effect.

2 *Environment* – an approach that relies on retail store atmospherics, on impressive architecture, on the power of space, place and *genius loci* (Sherry, 1998): the Niketown phenomenon, in other words.

3 *Esthetic* – a stance that espouses art, beauty and design, everything from quirky Alessi kettles and psychedelic Apple iMacs to day-glo Dyson vacuums and the 'feel' of a Mount Blanc pen (Dickinson and Svensen, 2000). Art for mart's sake, so to speak.

4 *Entertainment* – an acknowledgement that every business is show business. Hype, hoopla, headline-hogging are the order of the day. Make 'em laugh. Make 'em cry. Make 'em buy (Wolf, 1999). Richard Branson for beginners, basically.

5 *Ephemeral* – a net-driven notion based on buzz-building, fad-forwarding, chat-room churning, brand community boosting and unleashing the ideavirus (Godin, 2000; Rosen, 2000). In the beginning was the word of mouth, as it were.

6 *Evangelical* – an approach that taps into the oft-commented-on spirituality of consumption. It ranges from the use of religious iconography in advertising to finding the meaning of life in a bucket of Ben & Jerry's (Cohen and Greenfield, 1997; Weinreich, 1999).

7 *Ethical* – a standpoint predicated on Anita Roddick's (2001) credo of trade-not-aid and eco-conscious consumer behaviour. Just say no to rapaciousness, exploitation and waste. Buy a blusher, save the world (or the whales, at least).

8 *Effrontery* – shock sells, who bares wins, gross is good (Brown, 2001a): Benetton and so on and so on. If you don't want to fcuk me, fcuk off. Do I have to spell it out for you, you fcukers?

E-type marketing is many and varied, yet its espousers and enthusiasts share the belief that it is time for a change. Nowhere is this ebullient ethos better illustrated than in John Grant's (1999) *New Marketing Manifesto*. 'New Marketing', he argues, is predicated on creativity; it treats brands as living ideas; it is incorrigibly entrepreneurial; it favours change over conservatism; it is driven by insight, not analysis; and, above all, it is humanist in spirit rather than 'scientific':

> New Marketing is a challenge to the pseudo-scientific age of business. It is a great human, subjective enterprise. It is an art. New Marketing needs New Market Research. Old market research was largely there to objectify and to justify – to support conventions. New Marketing is here to challenge and seek the unconventional. (Grant, 1999, p. 182)

All very radical, you think, but not exactly novel. In fact, Grant's final chapter reveals that New Marketing is not so new after all: it is actually a reversion to the old style marketing – 'big inspiring, participative marketing', he terms it (p. 241) – that built up the megabrands of the early twentieth century (Kellogg's, Coca-Cola, Budweiser and so on), many of which are still going strong a century or so later. Old, it would seem, is the new new. Nostalgia is no longer a thing of the past, and what goes around, comes around.

In fairness, the self-same, same-old, same-old criticism could be levelled at all eight E-mergent schools of marketing thought. Patent medicine purveyors were the experiential marketers of the late nineteenth century (Lears, 1994); Marshall Field was a past master of in-store environment creation (Leach, 1993); Maxfield Parrish espoused marketing aesthetics before Philip Kotler was born (Bogart, 1995); P.T. Barnum was entertaining customers prior to the American Civil War (Cook, 2001); the history of marketing ephemerality reveals that it is anything but (door-to-door selling, periodic markets, itinerant peddlers, etc.); the ambulatory evangelists of antebellum America's 'Great Awakening' were the first modern marketing men (Moore, 1994); the 'truth in advertising' movement, an ethical eschewal of hard sell tactics, predates the First World War (Laird, 1998); and effrontery has long been a feature of marketer activity, as the 'invention' of BO (body odour), halitosis, housemaid's knee and analogous aliments reminds us (Marchand, 1985). Even the rise of consumerism is not exactly new. Three previous waves of anti-marketing sentiment have been identified by historically-minded researchers – 1960s, 1930s, 1900s – which imply the existence of a thirty-year (generational?) cycle in consumer activism (Hollander and Singh, 1994). In this regard, it is striking that the Battle of Seattle and subsequent anti-marketing 'carnivals' are constantly compared to the Paris street demonstrations of the 1960s. As one review of the year 2000 observed, 'Y2K was like 1968 revisited with online hacktivists, guerrilla gardeners and anarchist armies battling the forces of global capitalism from London's Mayday ruck to Prague's IMF summit' (Uncut, 2001, p. 46).

Step two: look back

It is, of course, entirely appropriate that marketing commentators should be espousing new versions of old ideas. It chimes with the times. It is in keeping with today's much-remarked upon (by me at least) 'retromarketing revolution'. One of the most striking marketing trends of recent years has been the abandonment of the new-and-improved, washes-whiter, we-have-the-technology mentality and the espousal of a golden-oldie, as-good-as-always, like-mother-used-to-make worldview (Brown, 2001a,b,c). A glance across the marketing landscape reveals that retro goods and services are all around. Old-fashioned brands, such as Atari, Airstream and Action Man have been adroitly revived and successfully relaunched. Ostensibly extinct trade characters, such as Mr Whipple, Morris the Cat and Charlie the Tuna, are cavorting on the supermarket shelves once more. Ancient commercials are being re-broadcast (Ovaltine, Alka-Seltzer); time-worn slogans are being resuscitated (Britney Spears sings 'Come Alive' for Pepsi); and long-established products are being re-packaged in their original, eye-catching liveries (Blue Nun, Sun Maid raisins). Even motor cars and washing powder, long the apotheosis of marketing's onward-and-upward ethos, are getting in on the retrospective act, as the success of the BMW Mini Cooper and Colour Protection Persil daily remind us (Hedberg and Singh, 2001).

The service sector, similarly, is adopting a time-was ethos. Retro casinos, retro restaurants, retro retail stores, retro holiday resorts, retro home pages and retro theme parks (with retro roller coasters) are two a penny. The movie business is replete with prequels, sequels and remakes (and, indeed, prequels of sequels of remakes such as the *Mummy III*), to say nothing of 'historical' spectaculars and post-modern period pieces such as *Moulin Rouge* and *Lord of the Rings*. *The Producers*, *Kiss Me Kate*, *Rocky Horror* and similar revivals are keeping the theatrical flag flying. Meanwhile, television programming is so retro that I-remember-the-day-before-yesterday's-weather-forecast cannot be far away. The music business, what is more, is retro a-go-go. Michael Jackson makes an invincible comeback. Madonna goes on tour again, after an eight-year hiatus. The artist formerly known as Prince is known as Prince, as before. Bruce Springsteen reconvenes the E-Street Band. Simple Minds are promising another miracle. Robbie Williams sings Sinatra. And U2 reclaim their title as the best U2 tribute band in the world. It is a beautiful payday.

Now, this is not to suggest that retro is the be all and end all of 21st-century marketing or that every sector is equally in thrall to the way we were. On the contrary, there is considerable variation in the 'depth' and 'breadth' of retro marketing. With regard to depth, for example, it is possible to distinguish between *Repro*, exact reproductions of old products, brands, packaging, promotional campaigns or whatever (e.g., Levi's Vintage range of retro apparel); *Repro Nova*, striking combinations of old-fashioned styling with state of the art technology (retro autos such as the Chrysler PT Cruiser); and *Repro de Luxe*, where different epochs are amalgamated anachronistically and past piled upon past until time topples over (the recently reanimated *Star Wars* saga).

In terms of 'breadth', it is clear that the penetration of retro varies from market to market. It has been suggested, for instance, that the gift-giving sector is especially susceptible to retro products, retro packaging, retro wrapping paper and all the rest (Samuel, 1994). The same is true, to some extent, of own-brand merchandise, insofar as supermarket own labels do not have the lineage of, say, Heinz, Nabisco or Kellogg's, and overcompensate with ostentatiously antiquated package designs (Brown, 2001a). Retro, likewise, seems to have been enthusiastically embraced in markets, such as apparel and entertainment, where the fashion cycle is especially swift and what little heritage there is is repeatedly raked over and reconfigured (Lehmann, 2000). The tasteful mail order catalogues of Martha Stewart, Ralph Lauren and Restoration Hardware, amongst others, also testify to the fact that home furnishings is a hotbed of retro (Franklin, 2002).

Yet regardless of variations in breadth and depth, perhaps the most striking thing about the retro revolution is its sheer ubiquity, such that it is hard to think of an unaffected product category. Retro radios, retro refrigerators, retro telephones, retro T-shirts, retro T-Birds, retro locomotives, retro lawnmowers, retro motor bikes, retro pogo sticks, retro sports equipment, retro ghetto blasters, retro garden furniture, retro wrist watches, retro writing instruments, retro computer games, retro cookery books, retro coffeepots, retro cosmetics, retro candles, retro comics, retro colas, retro cigarillos, retro cruise liners; the list is endless. As the acerbic comedian George Carlin (1997, p. 110) cogently contends:

> America has no now. We're reluctant to acknowledge the present. It's too embarrassing.
>
> Instead, we reach into the past. Our culture is composed of sequels, reruns, remakes, revivals, reissues, re-releases, re-creations, re-enactments, adaptations, anniversaries, memorabilia, oldies radio, and nostalgia record collections. World War Two has been refought on television so many times, the Germans and Japanese are now drawing residuals.
>
> Of course, being essentially full of shit, we sometimes feel the need to dress up this past-preoccupation, with pathetic references to reruns as 'encore presentations'.
>
> Even instant replay is a form of token nostalgia: a brief visit to the immediate past for re-examination, before slapping it onto a highlight video for further review and re-review on into the indefinite future.
>
> Our 'yestermania' includes fantasy baseball camps, where aging sad sacks pay money to catch baseballs thrown by men who were once their heroes. It is part of the fascination with sports memorabilia, a 'memory industry' so lucrative it has attracted counterfeiters.
>
> In this the Age of Hyphens, we are truly retro-Americans.

Step three: move together

The retro marketing revolution is all very well, but where is its critical edge? Is there one? Retro, surely, is reactionary rather than radical, is it not? In order to answer these questions it is necessary to reflect briefly on the nature of retro's appeal and consider what it is about retro goods and services that attracts 21st-century consumers. Clearly, the rise and rise of retro has something to do with nostalgia, consumers' yearning for the fondly remembered merchandise of their gilded youth, the wares they grew up with and remain favourably disposed towards, even if the products have long since departed for the great brand cemetery in the sky (Holbrook and Schindler 1994, 1996). It is surely no accident that the latter-day advent of retro marketing coincided with the communal mid-life crisis of the baby boom generation, who are increasingly inclined to cast backward glances at those long gone, late lamented days when bodies were firm, tummies were flat and follicles unchallenged. In today's hi-tech, hi-spec, high-speed world, where people are expected to keep moving, keep improving, keep one step ahead of the competition, it is hardly surprising that they pine for the days – and the products – when life was simpler, slower paced and less stressful (or so our rose-tinted, sepia-hued, soft-focused and completely unreliable memories suggest).

Retro marketing, however, is not just about appealing to consumers' warm and fuzzy yearnings for the way things were not, important though that is; its take-off is also attributable to retro's insidious softening of the hard sell. The golden glow of nostalgia, albeit ersatz nostalgia, renders marketing activities less rapacious than they ordinarily appear. It is again surely no accident that sectors traditionally associated with fast-talking, close-the-deal, watch-your-wallet flim-flam, such as property, financial services and motor cars, have been swift to board the retro marketing bandwagon. Estate agents and builders routinely boast of their illustrious heritage (established 1995, etc.); financial service providers consistently claim to have been faithfully serving the community for generations (calculated in canine years, naturally); and motor car manufacturers increasingly take their cue from a faux-golden age of motoring, when traffic congestion was unheard of, petrol prices were inconsequential and sitting behind the wheel was an allegedly unalloyed pleasure (where *do* the advertising agencies find all those empty roads?).

Retro goods and services, in short, disingenuously allude to a time *before* high-pressure sales tactics were the norm, *before* marketing was everywhere, *before* everything was completely, crassly, contemptibly commercialized. As Harris (2000, p. 49) sagely observes:

> To undercut the rising consumer awareness of the pitfalls of mass production and the chicanery of PR, companies calculatingly reject the seductive gimmicks of modem advertising and plaster their products with stodgy old women whose studied lack of glamour and sex appeal suggests that their product can appeal to the consumer on its own merits, without the help of Madison Avenue.

Retro, then, cunningly appeals to consumers' anti-marketing sentiments. Today's marketers, admittedly, like to think of themselves as customer-orientated, caring-sharing, you-rang-sir, servants-of-the-people; the good guys; the deliverers of a standard of living; the builders of a better tomorrow; the best a man can get (and then some). But consumers do not see things like that: quite the opposite, in point of fact. According to Goulding (2002), who has carried out a detailed empirical study of retro retail stores, consumers regard such establishments as 'authentic', as 'uncommercial', as a space that the market has not penetrated and despoiled. Buying goods in retro emporia represents a form of consumer resistance, a repudiation of high street chain stores, with their identikit, couldn't-care-less, next-customer-please, show-me-the-money attitude.

High street retailers, admittedly, hardly represent the cutting-edge of customer relationship management (CRM). However, we should not assume that, even if such organizations saw the light and became paragons of customer care, consumers would suddenly come to their senses and recognize that they were wrong about marketers all along; it is not going to happen. Consumers will *never* completely trust marketers, no matter how much we protest our innocence or insist that we are working in the customer's best interest. If anything, in fact, consumer scepticism is *increased* by improvements in marketing technology (ever-more personalized mail shots, specifically tailored, tweaked and targeted special offers, etc.), since the spectre of Hidden Persuaders is always hovering in the background. It is common knowledge – a veritable urban myth – that 'they' have ways of making us buy (Robinson, 1998; Butler *et al.*, 1999; Rushkoff, 1999). As David Letterman recently confessed, 'I don't believe in subliminal advertising. Then again, I went shopping yesterday and bought a combine harvester!'

Step four: hold tight

In addition to getting marketers of the marketing hook – until such times as consumers see through the ploy – retro raises a number of critical academic issues. The first of these concerns scholarly attempts to explain the retro marketing phenomenon. The rise of retro is more than a manifestation of the baby boomers' mid-life anxieties or marketers' anti-marketing inclinations. According to Stern (1992) it is attributable to the *fin de siècle* effect, humankind's propensity to cast a backward glance at the turn of centuries and millennia (Baudrillard, 1994; Bull, 1995). On the surface at least, the evidence is compelling, since a retrospective perspective was clearly apparent at the end of the 16th, 17th, 18th and 19th centuries, to say nothing of the year 1000 (Briggs and Snowman, 1996).

Closer inspection, however, reveals that the *fin de siècle* thesis does not withstand close scrutiny (Brown, 1999). While there is no doubt that the current millennial transition is characterized by retromania, the commodification of nostalgia is not confined to centuries' end; on the contrary, it is ever-present. The recent 1970s revival, for example, overlooks the fact that the 1970s were retro marketing minded (Frum, 2000). It was in the 1970s that Ridley Scott's sublime sepia-hued advertisement for Hovis was first broadcast. It was in the 1970s that *Brideshead Revisited* revitalized the British heritage industry, much to the annoyance of historical purists (Hewison, 1987). And it was in the 1970s that the Laura Ashley 'look', itself a revival of William Morris's medieval revivalism, took the nation's high streets by storm. The 1930s, likewise, were imbued with nostalgia marketing, all the way from Frank Lloyd Wright's 'Broadacre City', a futuristic attempt to revive Thomas Jefferson's neo-feudal fantasy of self-sustaining villages, to American consumers' propensity to decorate their dwellings with pewter tankards, spinning wheels and pseudo-Colonial artefacts (Lears, 1994). The late 19th century, what is more, also witnessed a rash of retro marketing. Many of the earliest mass-produced packaged goods were decorated with nostalgic images of a pre-lapsarian arcadia and many first-generation trade characters were blessed with a well of traditional, home-spun wisdom (Sivulka, 1998). The packaging of Hershey's chocolate, Quaker Oats, Keillor's Marmalade and Coca-Cola was retro to start with, though few surpassed the Nabisco orb and cross logo of 1901, which was adapted from a fifteenth-century Venetian printer's mark and is still in use today (Hine, 1995).

Another explanatory possibility is postmodernism (pardon my French). Now, postmodernism is one of the most ubiquitous buzzwords of our time, seemingly applied to everything from making love (over the Internet by means of teledildonic body-suits) to making war (where virtual missile strikes are mounted and computer hackers attack the software underbelly of their enemies). Inevitably, this has given rise to long lists of purportedly postmodern features or characteristics, which have themselves been much debated and discussed (S. Brown, 1995, 1998). It is generally accepted, however, that retrospection is an integral part of the postmodern condition. Postmodernism presupposes that stylistic innovation is impossible, that everything has already been tried, often several times over, and all that remains is to mix, match and play with the pieces of the past (ironically, naturally).

Although retro is often held up as a manifestation of porno, it is important to appreciate that the latter does not constitute an 'explanation' of the former (it is a homology at best or a tautology at worst). Postmodernism, after all, cannot account for the fact that retro marketing long predates the postmodern epoch. The Marlboro cowboy was retro from day one, as was Disney's Main Street USA (Bryman, 1995). 19th-century snake-oil sellers often maintained that their patent medicines were predicated on time-worn secrets of the ancients (Young, 1992). Josiah Wedgwood, the much-lauded prototype of marketing orientation, was himself a retro marketer. Many of his best-selling lines were replicas or 'contemporary' interpretations of classical themes (McKendrick, 1982). Set against this, it can of course be contended that postmodernism has been around for a very long time, under the guise of Romanticism, Anachronism and the anti-Enlightenment (Barzun, 2000). And so the debatable debate continues. The essential point, however, is that retro and porno are part and parcel of the same anti-establishment worldview.

A second critical issue arising out of retromania pertains to established marketing principles, inasmuch as the marketer's tried and tested toolkit looks and feels very different when examined from a retrospective perspective. When a retro posture is adopted towards the New Product Development (NPD) process, for example, it forcefully reminds us that the majority of marketer activity actually involves 'old product development'. As Cooper (1998) notes, new-to-the-world products represent a tiny fraction of NPD. The vast bulk of successful new product launches comprise line, brand and range extensions, coupled with product improvements, modifications or reformulations. Yet the process is not only called 'new product development' – a misnomer if ever there was one – but it also carries pejorative connotations, inasmuch as it implies that line extensions and so on are poor relations of 'proper' NPD. They are hackneyed, conservative, unimaginative and indicative of lazy managers, and a lack of marketing creativity.

Such an attitude, albeit very much in keeping with 'modern' marketing's imperishably progressive, shoulders-of-giants, to-infinity-and-beyond mindset, is one of the reasons why so many new-to-the-world products fail spectacularly in the marketplace. The notion of Old Product Development, on the other hand, makes eminent sense, since it initiates change but minimizes risk. It exploits the most underrated, understated and underutilized marketing resource of all, the presence of deep, powerful and long-established links between products and their consumers. Whether it be the new Beetle, *Star Wars Part I*, or Caffrey's Irish Ale, 'old' new products have a rich heritage to tap into, something that 'new' new products conspicuously lack. This is not to suggest that 'new' new product development be abandoned: far from it. But it emphasizes that marketers are primarily engaged in Old Product Development. It reminds us that new products are the exception rather than the rule. It suggests that the principal problem plaguing practitioners nowadays is not marketing myopia, but marketing amnesia.

The Product Life Cycle (PLC), perhaps the most venerated conceptual weapon in marketing's theoretical arsenal, is equally ripe for a retro-oriented reconfiguration. The traditional model posits a four-stage sequence of birth, growth, maturity and decline, though these stages are not clear-cut, their duration is indeterminate and their manageability is moot. Product life cycles, furthermore, are embedded within larger market life cycles that are made up, in turn, of individual brand and sub-brand life cycles. Yet, despite these variations, the PLC posits an inexorable, four-stage sequence that unfailingly ends with the end of the product concerned. Some ends come quickly, as with fads, fashions and cults, while other ends are deferred almost indefinitely, as the longevity of leading brands such as Coca-Cola and Marlboro happily attest. But the end cannot be prevented, according to the traditional model; it can only be postponed (Kotler, 2000).

When a retro stance is taken, however, it is evident that the Product Life Cycle concept should be replaced with the idea of a Product Life Circle, where the end is the beginning, where spring follows winter, where products are capable of rising, phoenix-like, from the ashes again and again and again. The risen product, furthermore, is recognizably the same, but it is refreshed, it is revitalized, it is potentially immortal rather than a candidate for termination. The beauty of the Product Life Circle concept is that, whereas the original, new-and-disproved PLC encouraged executives to kill off products unnecessarily, the old-and-improved PLC is irrepressibly optimistic. Renewal, revival and rejuvenation are perpetual possibilities; hope springs eternal, and a new day will dawn. It follows, therefore, that far from representing a regression, or the last gasp of marketing creativity, retro marketing represents redemption, a means of moving forwards, of going backwards into the future.

This is not the place to retrofit the pantheon of marketing principles, fascinating though that might prove. It is sufficient to note a third critical implication of the retro marketing revolution: namely, the history of the field itself. Retro suggests that instead of looking to the *guru du jour* – the E-mergent Eight referred to earlier, for example – marketers should seek inspiration in the *guru du hier* (so to speak), the intellectual giants of yesteryear, those who bestrode the discipline before the 'modern' marketing revolution of Kotler, Levy, Levitt *et al*. Retro suggests that rather than continue to await the arrival of a marketing Mendel, Einstein or Darwin, someone who has finally cracked the commercial code and unravelled the laws of the marketplace, it might be better to rummage in our dog-eared archives, dusty store cupboards and half-forgotten filing cabinets. Retro suggests, as an overenthusiastic retro marketer once put it, 'that there might be any number of cryogenised concepts deep frozen in the tundra of early 20th century marketing texts which could be successfully thawed out and reanimated' (Brown, 1999, p. 8).

In this regard, consider the cerebral iceberg that is Wroe Alderson, a once titanic marketing thinker who is now largely unread and, in truth, almost unreadable (Brown, 2002); yet, on working through Wroe's recondite writings, one cannot help but be struck by the prescience of his thought. Many of the issues, themes and concerns that marketing academics have addressed in the past half-century are anticipated in Alderson (Holbrook, 2001). Relationships, consumerism, societal marketing, not-for-profit, space and place, aesthetics, hedonics, demarketing, brand symbolism, product constellations, dark-side concerns, services marketing, internal marketing, self-marketing, the broadening debate, introspection as a research method, the market driving/driven dialectic and the extension of consumption to include post-purchase and disposition activities are all grist to the Aldersonian mill, as are re-engineering, just-in-time production, direct product profitability, total quality management and, believe it or not, the advent of e-commerce:

> Looking at the system as a whole, it is clear that the cost of carrying inventory should be kept to a moderate figure by starting just in time to prepare the inventory for the next season. Many considerations go into the phrase 'just in time', but the longer goods are in process or in storage, the higher the carrying charges will be. (Alderson and Green, 1964, p. 577)

> The time may come when two-way television and other electronic developments will make it possible to conclude many transactions without either buyer or seller leaving his regular location. (Alderson, 1957, p. 318)

What is more, the cryptic corpus of this 1950s futurologist is full of intriguing asides, parenthetical postulates and throw-away remarks, many of which remain eminently researchable. To cite but a single instance, in the penultimate chapter of *Dynamic Marketing Behavior*, Alderson (1965) introduces the idea of Undercover systems, consisting of the Underground (communist conspirators, etc.) and the Underworld (organized crime, in the main). For Wroe, the trade in proscribed goods and services, the payment of protection money and the dissemination of anti-capitalist ideas – let alone the links between these clandestine operations and legitimate systems such as households, enterprises and government bodies – are all potentially fruitful areas of marketing inquiry. *They still are*, as the drugs trade, Enron scandal, illegal immigrant transshipments and anti-capitalist riots in Seattle and suchlike attest.

Alderson is one such scholarly possibility, and Benjamin is another. To be sure, Walter Benjamin was not a fully paid up marketer: the complete opposite, in actual fact. He was a critical theorist, an affiliate of the influential Frankfurt School, which was founded in the inter-war era, transplanted itself in the USA during the Second World War, and returned to Germany in 1949. Unlike most incumbents of the Frankfurt School, whose aestheticized neo-Marxism meant that they had little time for popular culture, let alone the accoutrements of capitalism, Benjamin had a soft spot for the marketing system. True, this sympathetic attitude may have stemmed from his family background (his father was a marketer), as well as his own business interests (a freelance writer without scholarly sinecure and subject to the vagaries of the literary marketplace, Benjamin kept the wolf from the door by dealing in antiquarian books), but his writings are suffused with references to the magic of the marketplace, as his awestruck encomium to an ad for Bullrich Salt brilliantly illustrates:

> Many years ago, on the streetcar, I saw a poster that, if things had their due in this world, would have found its admirers, historians, exegetes, and copyists just as surely as any great poem or painting. And, in fact, it was both at the same time. As is sometimes the case with very deep, unexpected impressions, however, the shock was too violent: the impression, if I may say so, struck with such force that it broke through the bottom of my consciousness and for years lay irrecoverable somewhere in the darkness. I knew only that it had something to do with 'Bullrich Salt' and that the original warehouse for this seasoning was a small cellar on Flottwell Street, where for years I had circumvented the temptation to get out at this point and inquire about the poster. There I traveled on a colorless Sunday afternoon ... [and] stood with my two beautiful companions in front of a miserable café, whose window display was enlivened by an arrangement of signboards. On one of these was the legend 'Bullrich Salt'. It contained nothing else but the words; but around these written characters there was suddenly and effortlessly configured that desert landscape of the poster. I had it once more. Here is what it looked like. In the foreground, a horse-drawn wagon was advancing across the desert. It was loaded with sacks bearing the words 'Bullrich Salt'. One of these sacks had a hole, from which the salt had already trickled a good distance on the ground. In the background of the desert landscape, two posts held a large sign with the words 'Is the Best'. But what about the trace of salt down the desert trail? It formed letters, and these letters formed a word, the word 'Bullrich Salt'. Was not the preestablished harmony of a Leibniz mere child's play compared to this tightly orchestrated predestination in the desert? And didn't that poster furnish an image for things that no one in this mortal life has yet experienced? An image of the everyday in Utopia? (Benjamin, 1999, pp. 173–4)

Alongside the art of advertising, Benjamin was fascinated by consumer behaviour in general and retro marketing in particular. He spent 14 years of his life gathering material for a book on the shopping arcades of 19th-century Paris and, although the text was never published, its rough notes reveal that he was obsessed with retro, with marketing, with old objects, with abandoned possessions, with superseded technologies, with long-forgotten fads and fashions, and the general flotsam and jetsam of the commercial system, all of which eventually washed up on the wind-swept, weather-beaten shores of the shopping arcades (Benjamin, 1999). The 19th-century Parisian arcades, in fact, were retro first and last:

> Just as there are places in the stones of the Miocene or Eocene Age that bear the impression of huge monsters out of these geological epochs, so today the Passages [Arcades] lie in the great cities like caves containing fossils of an ur-animal presumed extinct: The consumers from the pre-imperial epoch of capitalism, the last dinosaurs of Europe. (Buck-Morss, 1991, p. 65)

Step five: repeat

Here, then, is the ultimate irony of the contemporary marketing condition. It is being attacked on all sides. It is being attacked by Nike-wearing rioters throwing rocks at Niketown. It is being attacked by marketing commentators, who disdain old-style marketing management but whose E-type alternatives are even older still. It is being attacked by contemporary critical theorists and post-modern fellow travellers, most of whom hold professorships in business schools and are themselves in thrall to the capitalist system they condemn. Even Philip Kotler (1999), the founding father of the modern marketing concept, has recently come out against the APIC paradigm, the very framework that he formulated and, thanks to his proselytizing endeavours, that has dominated the field for 40-odd years!

Meanwhile, marketing has never been so popular among sociologists, anthropologists, geographers, historians and all the rest. Their journals abound with insightful analyses of shopping centres, department stores, brand communities, global marketing strategies and so forth. They possess a roster of gifted thinkers, such as Walter Benjamin, whose marketing-rich, marketing-relevant, marketing-replete theories have been largely ignored by 'proper' marketing academics and researchers (noteworthy exceptions include Heilbrunn, 1998, and Belk, 2002). Similarly, the most creative marketing practitioners these days – Damien Hirst, Tracey Emin, Madonna, Max Clifford, Puff Daddy – are people who remain untainted by marketing principles of the 4 Ps variety and whose success stems from the fact that they *haven't* been trained in business schools with their me-too modules, me-too textbooks and me-too Masters of Business Administration degrees (Brown and Patterson, 2000).

Nowhere is this inversion better illustrated than in the case of Naomi Klein, of *No Logo* fame. She has brilliantly marketed her brand of anti-marketing by intimating that her much-marketed book is a marketing-free zone. The very fact that she has trademarked the No Logo logo suggests that an acute marketing sensitivity is at work. Today's consumers, however, are not so easily fooled. Surely it will not be long before No Logo T-shirt-wearing protesters storm the offices of *No Logo*'s publisher and a best-selling book is written about the event: *No No Logo*, no doubt. Anyone for No No No Logo, No No No No Logo or No No No No No Logo?

Marketing, in sum, is not on the critical list; it is alive and well. It has escaped the business school and is back on the street where it belongs. Respect.

Chapter 9

The future of marketing

jagdish n. sheth and rajendra s. sisodia

Aims

In this chapter, we describe the ongoing transformation of the marketing function from a product- and market-centred perspective to a customer-centred perspective. We will discuss how marketing's focus is shifting from anonymous market transactions to personalized customer interactions. Implicit in this shift is the opportunity to achieve better profitability by treating customers differently and by reducing cross-customer subsidies. We then discuss how customer-centred marketing requires marketers to transcend customer satisfaction to achieve customer commitment, and how this is only possible if marketers shift their focus from creating tactical marketing programmes to designing strategic business processes. Next, we describe how companies can implement customer-centred marketing by doing the following: focusing on creating end-user value; using cross-functional teams; implementing automation and integration; using 'fixed cost' marketing; viewing marketing as supply management; creating profit and loss (P&L) accountability for marketing; creating a subscription model of marketing; and bringing marketing and business development together. We conclude by looking at some emerging issues facing the practice of customer-centred marketing.

Introduction

Marketing as a function and profession has been undergoing a fundamental shift over the past several years. In the early 1990s, students of marketing – be they managers, academics or consultants – started to realize that there were many deep-seated problems with the field that could not be addressed through incrementalism; addressing these would require the adoption of a radically different approach to how marketing is organized and conceptualized. This chapter is about how marketing in the future is likely to be shaped by this new thinking.

The state of the function

Evidence abounds of growing cynicism among customers, even as companies have invested billions of dollars implementing ambitious customer relations management (CRM) automation projects in the hope that they would thereby transform themselves into customer-focused enterprises. Customers' trust in the marketing function is perhaps as low as it has ever been; especially in the consumer market, few consumers regard themselves as truly being in a relationship with the companies they do business with. For example, a recent survey by the UK-based Marketing Forum/Consumers' Association found the following (Mitchell, 2001):

- 83 per cent of consumers agreed with the statement that 'As a consumer, companies just see me as someone with money to spend.'

- 76 per cent agreed that 'Many companies see their brands as a way of pushing up prices.'

- 78 per cent agreed that 'Companies like to pretend that their brands are really different, but actually there's rarely any substantial difference between them.'

- 70 per cent agreed that 'I don't trust most advertising of products or services because they're just trying to sell me something.'

These numbers should not be surprising to anyone in the marketing profession; most seem resigned to the fact that their profession is generally held in low esteem by its primary constituents, the customers it seeks to acquire and keep.

One hopes that marketers have earned the respect of their colleagues from other functional areas, who at least recognize the difficulty of their challenges? Wrong! A survey of how executives from other business functions view the performance of their marketing colleagues found the following (Heeringa, 1998) to be the case.

- Only 38 per cent rated their marketing colleagues as good or excellent
- Only 18 per cent considered marketing executives to be results-orientated (while 71 per cent of the marketers perceived themselves in that manner)
- Only 34 per cent viewed marketers as strategic thinkers

What does this tell us (other than the fact that the self-esteem of marketers is remarkably impervious to erosion)? We strongly believe that it indicates the following:

- Marketing is more vital to business success than ever, but 'marketing-as-usual' is expensive and increasingly ineffective, alienating more customers than it satisfies
- The biggest opportunity for corporations to improve financial performance lies in the marketing department
- This does *not* mean that companies should throw money and technology at the problem (in the form of huge deployments of CRM software, typically at an incremental cost of several thousand dollars per year per marketer)
- Rather, it requires several fundamental shifts: in mindset, corporate culture, compensation and reward systems, and perhaps terminology

The fundamental shift in marketing

The fundamental shift in marketing is from market-centred transactions to customer-centred interactions, as depicted in Figure 9.1.

Most schools of marketing thought until recently have centred on market transactions. The focus has been on the market as a whole or segments within markets, and the measurement techniques used have dealt with market transactions. Under this paradigm, marketers view customers as objects (some would even suggest 'prey') to be targeted and conquered. Communication with the customer is strictly one-way, and is centred on product features and benefits, with the objective of creating a transaction on terms favourable to the marketer.

The focus now has to shift from *markets to customers*, and from *transactions to interactions*, a dual transformation from current generation marketing to next generation marketing. Marketing is thus headed towards interaction and customer focus.

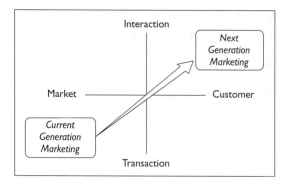

Figure 9.1   The fundamental shift in marketing

The importance of customer interactions has increased dramatically with the overwhelming dominance of the service sector in all developed economies, and the trend towards a growing services sector even in developing countries. Interactions are ubiquitous in a service economy, and the techniques and traditions of marketing must reflect this shift.

On the other side, we see the diminished significance of the collective market and the rising importance of the individual customer. This has been accentuated by the growing diversity among customer ranks; today, there is greater age, income, life-style and ethnic diversity than ever before, rendering mass marketing largely obsolete. Further, emerging communication and interaction technologies have made it economically viable to address and respond to customers individually. Marketing is thus fundamentally shifting towards customer-centred or customer interaction marketing and away from transaction marketing.

What is customer-centred marketing?

Customer-centred marketing, as we define it, is the ongoing collaborative business activities between a supplier and a customer on a one-to-one basis for the purpose of creating better, cheaper and faster end-user value. An important and essential characteristic of customer-centred marketing is that by delivering better end-user value, companies ultimately also deliver better shareholder value.

In customer-centred marketing, marketers assess each customer *individually* and make a determination of whether to serve that customer directly, via a third party or not at all. Also, customer-centred marketers must determine whether to create an offering that customizes the product and/or some other element(s) of the marketing mix, or to standardize the offering. Their actions are guided by analysis intended to maximize the 'effective efficiency' of marketing actions (Sheth and Sisodia, 1995). Raising efficiency entails conducting a cost-benefit analysis, and maximizing the output to input ratio for individual customers. Effectiveness entails the enhancement of customer loyalty and growing the company's 'share of wallet'. The objective of customer-centred marketing is to maximize both efficiency and effectiveness simultaneously at the customer level.

Customer-centred marketing is distinct from 'one-to-one' marketing. Several authors have recently suggested that firms practise 'one-to-one' marketing through the use of mass customization (Peppers and Rogers, 1993; Pine, Victor and Boynton, 1993; Gilmore and Pine, 1997; Peppers, Rogers and Dorf, 1999). 'One-to-one' marketing focuses on the adaptation of product or offering (i.e., it is a product-centred approach) and makes the product the starting point of the planning process. In contrast, customer-centred marketing focuses on the needs, wants and resources of customers as the starting point of the planning process.

It is also important to delineate the linkages between customer-centred marketing and relationship marketing. To practise effective relationship marketing, companies must have a customer-centred focus. The converse is generally not true, since companies can engage in customer-centred marketing without practising relationship marketing. Transactional customer-centred marketing occurs often in direct marketing situations where the level of customer involvement and interest in an interactive relationship is low. Also, as we discuss below, customer-centred marketing may lead to the outsourcing of customers, which clearly is not the same as relationship marketing.

How we got here: the evolution of marketing practice and philosophy

Over time, marketing practice and philosophy has evolved from a highly product-centred view to one centred on competitive forces and is now moving towards a customer-centred orientation.

For many decades, marketing was primarily about how best to promote and package products. Companies focused on product differentiation, product availability and price advantage. Branding was central: everything revolved around the brand. This was especially the case in business-to-business contexts; if a company was good at making a product, the only value added by marketing was to create access through the use of distribution channels and establishing awareness for the product.

Following this, marketing went through a cycle of becoming intensely competition-centred, especially in the 1970s and 1980s. Having enjoyed a seller's market earlier, many companies were now confronted with excess capacity. The central issue for them became how they could compete in the crowded marketplace, especially with the rise in global competition. In order to combat the tendency towards commoditization, companies adopted strategies such as low cost, differentiation and focused positioning relative to competitors.

While customers initially benefit from heightened competitive intensity, too much competition can lead to high levels of inefficiency, especially in marketing. Companies strive to match and outdo each other in terms of trade wars, price wars and advertising wars, with little to show in return in terms of increased revenues (especially in mature industries) or customer loyalty. Gradually, companies have come to realize that too much competition can destroy them. They are now looking to use the customer rather than competition as the primary basis for strategizing and positioning.

The strategic advantages of customer-centred marketing

As pointed out above, an important reason for the fundamental shift towards customer-centred marketing is that the way marketing is currently organized and managed is not very productive. One way in which customer-centred marketing can be more productive is that customers often become part of the marketer's value chain. As a result, some costs are shifted to customers. For example, customers undertake most of the work when they interact with a company's web pages; they search for the information they need and input all the information that the marketer needs. Even in the physical world, most customers have embraced the trend towards greater self-service.

Marketing productivity is also enhanced through mutual learning on the part of marketers as well as customers. It is a well-known principle in physics that it is much harder to get a stationary object to start moving than it is to keep a moving object moving. In other words, 'static friction' greatly exceeds 'kinetic friction'. In most marketing, however, the customer relationship starts from a standstill position every time, and is thus subject to a high level of static friction. Experience curve effects (i.e., the benefits of mutual learning) are lacking, since every transaction is similar to the first transaction. The marketer fails to become more efficient and effective in meeting the customer's needs over time; likewise, customers continue to perform like novices in the relationship.

Another way in which customer-centred marketing leads to improved marking productivity is through the reduction or even elimination of cross-subsidies across customers that are built into the system. In most cases, companies may be unaware that they are subsidizing some customers at the expense of others, making the latter vulnerable to competitive poaching. Figure 9.2 shows that if a company's customers are ranked from largest to smallest, and if the company is able to appropriately determine the costs of serving each customer (e.g., through the use of activity-based costing), it would find that a small proportion of its customers are highly profitable, while many are downright unprofitable. Unless the company moves aggressively to establish strong relationships and hard-to-break bonds with its most profitable customers, it will soon discover that those customers are the first ones to be targeted by savvy competitors. The company must be willing to invest in these customers in direct proportion to their value; if made correctly, such investments should make these customers even more profitable than they were previously (Sheth, Sisodia and Sharma, 2000).

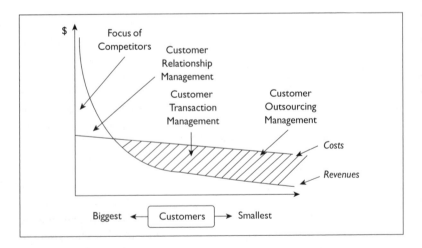

Figure 9.2   The strategic advantage of customer-centred marketing

The second tier of customers consists of those that are currently marginally profitable or marginally unprofitable. The third tier consists of customers that are clearly highly unprofitable. Marketers can pursue one of two strategies for how to treat unprofitable customers. The first is neglect, which leads to dissatisfied and alienated ex-customers and undesirable public relations consequences.

The second and more appropriate strategy is the outsourcing of customers (Sheth and Sisodia, 1999). Marketing has traditionally outsourced many of its functions to third parties (e.g., distribution, advertising, product design, market research), but not customers. The outsourcing of customers can take many forms. For example, a company may contract with an outside vendor to serve certain customers, a change that customers may not even be aware of. Alternatively, a company could sell its customer base to another company for a one-time fee or for a share of future revenues or profits.

Fundamentally, the logic of customer outsourcing is to make unprofitable customers profitable by making them a part of another company's more favourable cost structure. For example, a local telecommunications company that provides a bundle of services to customers is likely to make more profit on a low-volume long-distance customer than a company that only sells that customer long-distance service. The key is to identify competitor-partners for whom the outsourced customers could become part of a broader one-stop-shopping strategy.

Going beyond customer satisfaction

Until now, marketing has attempted to create satisfied customers through the creation of the 'right' marketing programme: that blend of marketing mix elements to which the customer is most likely to respond favourably (see Figure 9.3). However, most elements of these marketing mix programmes were aimed at the collective market or segment being targeted, rather than at specific customers. Moreover, they are heavily skewed in their emphasis towards the *initial* transaction, and little changes as the customer becomes more familiar with the company's offering after repeated purchases.

The most important issue is how companies can go beyond customer satisfaction and retain satisfied customers. This requires getting a commitment out of the customer. The marketing literature has placed too much emphasis on satisfying the customer; many companies are able to do so but lose a great deal of money in the process. The key to customer-centred

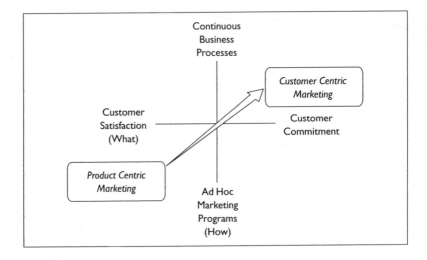

Figure 9.3   Customer-centred marketing: antecedents

marketing is that the relationship between company and customers is a two-way street, so that both parties have to benefit on a sustained basis. This requires commitment on both sides.

The second key dimensional shift is from *ad hoc* tactical marketing programmes towards the design of continuous business processes centred on optimizing an ongoing stream of customer interactions. The marketing mix as a concept is thus becoming increasingly obsolete; the focus is shifting to processes, and how a company can organize in the best way to retain its customers. The marketing mix is all about getting customers (usually in an undiscriminating and undisciplined manner), as long as they are part of a broadly defined target market. Customer-centred marketing, in contrast, is about acquiring, keeping and growing the *right* customers. It requires companies to undertake extensive diligence on customers and to have the courage to reject unsuitable ones. It also requires paying a great deal of attention to managing customer expectations so that satisfaction and commitment will result (Sheth and Mittal, 1996). Finally, it requires the development of mutually acceptable business processes that span firm boundaries and deliver quantum improvements in efficiency and effectiveness.

Unlike traditional selling, marketing is a long-term game. Selling is analogous to hunting, while marketing is becoming more like farming (Sawhney and Kotler, 1999). While the hunter is only concerned with setting the right bait and using the best weapon to take down his prey, the farmer takes a long-term view in which achieving sustainable results takes precedence over immediate gratification. The farmer plants the right seeds in the right kind of soil, nurtures the saplings through irrigation and fertilization, removes weeds that take away vital resources from the plants, and reaps a periodic harvest. Likewise, customer-centred marketing selects the right customers, helps them grow and thrive by making investments in serving them and weeding out parasitic, unprofitable customers, and takes periodic harvests in the form of profits. From these harvests come the seeds of future crops of customers, through favourable word-of-mouth as well as the resources and knowledge necessary to acquire additional profitable customers.

Despite the fact that marketing is a long-term game, marketing activities continue to be budgeted and organized as though they result in an immediate sale, rather than build an asset over time. The only way to change this is to shift the focus from programmes to processes. Companies should invest in processes with a view to getting long-term returns. This is also linked to the trend towards fixed cost marketing, which we discuss later in this chapter.

Thus far, we have outlined several reasons why marketing has to move towards customer-centred marketing. We now turn our attention to the issue of how companies can make the transition towards customer-centred marketing.

Operationalizing customer-centred marketing

In this section, we will discuss eight keys to operationalizing customer-centred marketing:

- focus on creating end-user value
- use cross-functional teams
- implement automation and integration
- use fixed-cost marketing
- view marketing as supply management
- create P&L accountability for marketing
- create a subscription model of marketing
- bring marketing and business development together

Focus on creating end-user value

The starting point for customer-centred marketing is the creation of superior end-user value. End-user value takes three forms: performance value, price value and personalization value (Mittal and Sheth, 2001).

As Figure 9.4 shows, 'performance value' derives from the maintenance of high-quality standards and continuous innovation. This enables the firm to deliver superior functional value compared to most of its competitors. 'Price value' comes from the use of target costing (resulting in price-based costing rather than cost-based pricing) and mass customization (the delivery of tailored solutions for approximately the same cost as mass-produced ones). This enables the firm to consistently deliver better price-performance to the customer. 'Personalization value' results from the use of frontline information systems (providing cutting-edge information technology tools to frontline employees as well as directly to customers), empowering competent employees to make decisions at the point of inter-action and the delivery of customer-demanded value added services.

Use cross-functional teams

Delivering superior end-user value also requires that a firm invest in new business processes that span the boundary between firm and customer. A prime example of this is the use of cross-functional teams to manage and grow customer relationships, a practice that is becoming increasingly

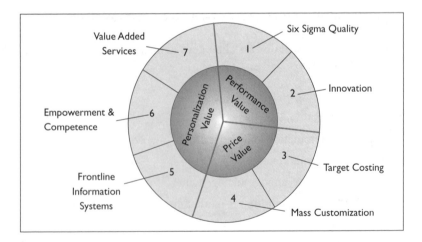

Figure 9.4 Customer-centred marketing focuses on end-user value

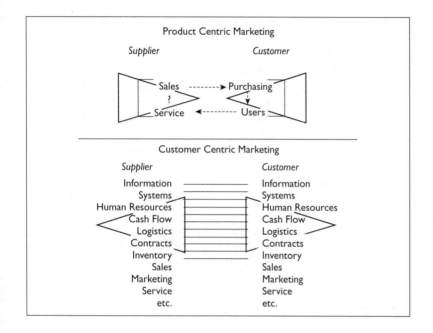

Figure 9.5 Product versus customer-centred marketing

widespread. Initially pioneered by Wal-Mart and Procter & Gamble (as depicted in Figure 9.5), such teams have now proliferated across the business-to-business landscape, especially for relationships deemed to be long-term strategic partnerships. As the figure indicates, these teams are comprised of individuals from a wide variety of functional areas within the company, interacting as a team with their counterparts from the customer firm. The teams can range in size from a few part-time individuals to a hundred or more members deployed full-time at the customer's site. For example, Procter & Gamble's team at Wal-Mart and Coca-Cola's team at McDonald's each comprise more than a hundred individuals.

Cross-functional teams epitomize the interaction aspect of customer-centred marketing. The role of marketing in cross-functional teams is at the centre as the co-ordinator. Most team members come from other functional areas, but it is marketing's job to serve as the quarterback and relationship nerve centre. Marketing in this context thus becomes a staff rather than line function; its job is orchestrating and co-ordinating the activities of the team, in addition to managing the customer relationship itself. The marketing budget is distributed across the orchestrated activities rather than being centralized within the marketing function.

Implement automation and integration

In order to implement customer-centred marketing efficiently and effectively, companies need to put into practice a great deal of automation and integration (Figure 9.6). Most companies can be characterized as consisting of location silos and time silos; there is insufficient communication and co-ordination between locations (which may be sites of different operations or functional activities), and there are also built-in structural delays between the recognition and fulfilment of internal and external needs. The 'connected enterprise' of the future will feature an integrated organization with no boundaries between locations, and the ability to offer automated 'real time' fulfilment of needs. This allows the company to present a single face to the customer with the promise of real-time attention to customer needs. For example, consider the computerized reservation systems (CRS) of major airlines: both operations and customers are on-line on a global basis, permitting real-time selling and capacity planning.

Use fixed-cost marketing

As marketing becomes more technology-intensive in the future, it will develop and leverage a widespread technology-based infrastructure, leading to what we call 'fixed-cost marketing'. In fixed-cost marketing, the marketing costs associated with serving an incremental customer are very low. Consequently, marketing practices exhibit stronger experience curve effects than they currently do as well as increasing returns to scale

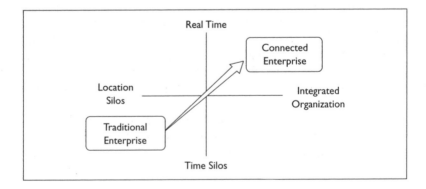

Figure 9.6   Customer-centred marketing requires
automation and integration

(rather than the diminishing returns to scale currently seen with most marketing activities).

The trend towards fixed-cost marketing parallels a broader shift that has taken place in society. In the agriculture age, most costs were variable, such as seed, water, fertilizer, labour, storage and transportation. The only fixed asset was land, which was usually inherited. In the industrial age, the total cost of doing business included sizeable fixed and variable components. This gave rise to the opportunity for firms to exploit economies of scale and scope; firms sought to spread their fixed costs over a larger volume. Average costs declined slowly with volume, and prevailing market prices tended to closely track production costs.

In the information age, costs are mostly fixed. The customer-centred marketing era will be the era of customer knowledge. In any knowledge-based industry, fixed costs dominate. Knowledge products (such as software, computer chips, and new drugs) tend to have very high upfront costs (research and development) and high fixed costs for plant and equipment but very low marginal costs of production.

Having a fixed-cost dominated marketing structure is tantamount to developing a marketing infrastructure in which everything that *can* be automated *is* automated. The costs of that infrastructure are largely invariant with respect to volume. Elements of the infrastructure can thus be profitably shared with other companies engaged in similar businesses or others targeting the same customers with complementary offerings. By sharing the costs, companies can develop infrastructures of virtually unlimited capacity and extremely low unit costs. Adding additional complementary products and services that would be of interest to the same customer group can then leverage the marketing system.

As it happens, the biggest infrastructure element today, the Internet, already exists and requires a relatively small expenditure to utilize. For this reason, we believe that we have only seen a small portion of the impact that the Internet will have on the marketing function.

Another implication of fixed-cost marketing is that since fixed costs are listed on the balance sheet, marketing becomes even more like a long-term investment as opposed to an annual expenditure.

View marketing as supply management

An important shift that occurs with the practice of customer-centred marketing is that marketing becomes akin to supply management. If customer interactions are the starting point, you must work backwards from the customer. In this form of 'reverse marketing', the role of marketing is to make sure that what the customer wants and needs (cheaper, better, faster) is delivered. The whole flow shifts: marketing becomes more about 'customer pull' and less about 'company push'. The company's focus shifts from 'finding customers for products' towards 'finding products for customers'.

Marketing thus becomes more like a systems integrator; if the customer wants a certain bundle of offerings, it is marketing's job to provide it, even if the company does not itself make all the elements of the bundle. This can be thought of as 'virtual integration', rather than vertical integration. Marketing becomes an extension of the customer's buying organization; in order to assemble the customer's desired bundle, marketing must in turn deal with suppliers who can provide the missing pieces. The procurement or purchasing function becomes a highly strategic activity for marketing, and a persuasive case can be made that it should report to marketing.

Taking on this greatly expanded role successfully – from a purveyor of individual products to a provider of broad solutions – requires that marketing become a 'trusted adviser' to the customer. In other words, the supplier's marketing function becomes the customer's agent and trusted buyer. It becomes a support and extension of customer's procurement process, and sources products and services that may or may not be produced by its own company. It shifts from the selling to the buying function. It may also lead firms occasionally to engage in merger and acquisition activity in order to be able to deliver more consistently certain often-requested components of the bundle to its customers.

Figure 9.7 shows how information technology plays into this. Enterprise resource planning (ERP) systems deal with the enhancement of back office productivity and leverage internal networks. These have typically been the focus on initial efforts by companies to embrace business automation. The focus then moved to further enhancing back office and 'upstream' productivity by linking with external supplies, which has been the focus of supply chain management systems. Companies in recent years have returned their focus to leveraging internal networks to deliver superior front line productivity in the form of CRM systems. The final stage in this evolution is to practise truly interactive marketing by simultaneously incorporating its customers and suppliers in an extranet.

The key message here is that the supply chain for a company pertains to more than manufacturing: it is a more generalized concept that is not usually understood in broad enough terms. Marketing already manages a number of external suppliers, for outsourced marketing functions such as market research, advertising, telemarketing, even product design.

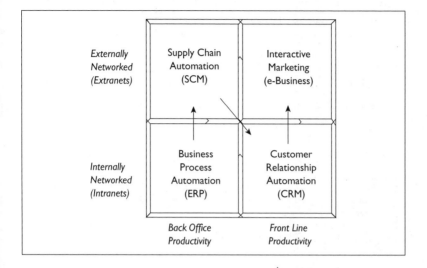

Figure 9.7   Emergence of CRM and e-business

As we suggest above, marketing also needs to manage the external supply chain for complementary products and services to those created in-house, in order to complete the bundles that customers desire.

Marketing also needs to take responsibility for managing internal suppliers, chief among which is the company's own operations. As we discuss below, this perspective leads logically to the need to separate marketing's P&L from that of a company's operational P&L.

Create P&L accountability for marketing

The effective implementation of customer-centred marketing requires breaking up the vertical P&L that is typically found in most companies (Figure 9.8). Most companies have business units in which operations, sales and marketing, and customer support/service are all together. Each business unit is managed as a P&L. Instead, companies should have two P&Ls: one for operations/manufacturing, the other for marketing (which includes sales and service). To implement this, companies should create a Chief Customer Officer (CCO) position with P&L responsibility comparable to the Chief Operating Officer (COO) position.

The CCO is not just a revenue generator but also a cost manager, so he/she has to deliver financial performance to the Chief Executive

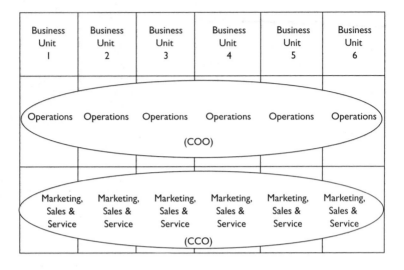

Figure 9.8 Customer-centred marketing requires P&L accountability

Officer (CEO). Toyota has already done this: it has a separate distribution company, which is a P&L entity. This approach has also been implemented recently at a leading telecommunications company, where the 'Network' is managed as one P&L and 'Customers and Markets' as another.

A key question that arises is the transfer price between operations and marketing, and this could be done in two ways. One is to allow the factory to make 'normal rents', not monopoly rents; the second (and preferred) way is to benchmark against competitors at the factory level. When marketing becomes organized customer-by-customer, it has to decide whether a product should be made in-house or bought from the outside. That requires that marketing be freed to buy from outside if the factory is not able to deliver value that is competitive with the marketplace.

Create a subscription model of marketing

More and more manufacturing companies such as IBM and General Electric are evolving into service companies. When this happens, customer focus and interaction become even more important. Companies tend to have more direct relationships with customers, rather than going through intermediaries.

An attractive option for any service company is to enter into a subscription-style relationship with its customers, in which the default state is for the relationship to continue uninterrupted unless the customer specifically initiates a service change or termination. For example, Microsoft has announced a subscription-based model for software, and Xerox and General Electric have embraced subscription-style models as well.

The attraction of this approach is based on the following points:

1   The installed product base for services keeps growing even if unit product sales are flat. For example, a company selling 10,000 units annually will have an installed base of 50,000 in five years (assuming that the life of the product exceeds five years). Over time, the economics of the business are heavily dependent on the installed base, rather than on new sales. Many companies make the mistake of attempting to make the bulk of their profits from the sale of new units rather than leveraging the installed base. With a subscription model of marketing, revenues and profits are explicitly tied to the growing installed base.

2   Core products and services are becoming commoditized, shifting the locus of competition towards service elements. Manufacturing is getting highly standardized as companies adopt open technology platforms and even share suppliers with their competitors. Companies therefore cannot expect to command high margins based on their products. However, services can and do deliver higher margins.

3   It creates an annuity model of revenues. Forecasting becomes a lot more stable. The ratio of fixed to variable revenues becomes higher (paralleling a similar shift in costs, as discussed earlier). The customer has rendered the 'make versus buy' decision in favour of buying, and has outsourced the provision of the function to the supplier on an indefinite basis.

4   It has great potential for win–win value creation, as both sides are able to come out ahead if it is done right. The customer has outsourced a non-core activity to a supplier for whom it is a core activity. Typically, customers can get 'more for less' under such a scenario, while the supplier reaps the benefits of specialization and economies of scale as higher profits.

5   It provides an opportunity for closer bonding between a company and its customers. The relationship is an ongoing one, and interactions

between the company and the customer focus on how new value can be created.

While many of the opportunities for subscription marketing are in the business-to-business domain, we see great growth potential in consumer markets. Many business-to-business companies in the past decade have moved towards the practice of 'automatic replenishment' or 'vendor-managed inventory', in which manufacturers take on the responsibility for managing inventory at the retail level. Monitoring starting inventory levels and sell-through volumes, manufacturers automatically ship additional merchandise when stock is depleted. The advantages of this approach are several: the frequency of stock 'outs' is greatly reduced, and many administrative costs associated with ordering, invoicing and billing are reduced or eliminated. Implemented effectively, this approach results in higher levels of product availability at the point of purchase with much lower average levels of inventory. The adoption rate for these approaches has been very strong; 80 per cent of retailers now use some form of automatic replenishment, and companies have reported up to 400 per cent increase in inventory turns and 75 per cent reduction in stock 'out' situations.

Beset with inefficient and ineffective marketing approaches, the consumer market is now ripe for the widespread deployment of this approach. We strongly believe that marketing efficiency as well as effectiveness in consumer markets can be greatly increased through the routinization and automation of purchase and consumption.

The automation of consumption, first and foremost, is aimed at simplifying life for buyers as well as sellers (Sheth and Sisodia, 2000). For example, buyers can be freed of the burden of monitoring inventory levels of frequently purchased goods. It is about understanding customers so deeply and thoroughly that marketers can anticipate their needs and wants, often even before the customers themselves are consciously aware of those needs and wants. It reflects a 'customer business development' mindset (which is becoming common in business marketing situations, as discussed in the next section) applied to the consumer market, wherein marketers and consumers continually look for opportunities to elevate the mutual gains from their relationship. It is, in brief, auto-pilot marketing, in which most human intervention may only be required at take-off (relationship creation) and landing (relationship termination, in the event that it ceases to make economic sense).

Our consumption-driven society is taking a heavy toll on many consumers, not because there is too much consumption but because of the additional burden it places on consumers seeking to make reasonably informed purchase decisions. With the widespread adoption of standardized production approaches such as TQM (total quality management) and ISO 9000, average product quality has improved, but so has the level of standardization and conformity across products. Even 'generic' products offer good quality and a high level of standardized capabilities. Consumers are thus faced with the prospect of engaging in a great deal of shopping behaviour (given the abundance of pseudo-choices and seemingly random price differentials across stores and over time) with little incremental value at stake. The result: the true 'ROI' (return on investment) on shopping effort is very low, given the amount of time and physical and mental effort expended and the high level of commoditization in many product categories.

Any alternative model, such as the automation of consumption, must be highly efficient in its use of all resources, not just time. It must also be built on a high level of mutual trust and respect, and the nearly-complete absence of opportunistic action by both sides.

The benefits of the automation of consumption can be summed up in Mobil's phrase in the advertisements for its Speed Pass service: it is 'like buying time without paying for it'. The automation of consumption can work with all kinds of products, including commodities. The key is that the experience must not be commoditized, even though the core products may well be.

Bring marketing and business development together

Marketing and the merging domain of 'business development' have to come together. The skill sets required are quite different, even more so than the differences in skill sets between sales and marketing.

In today's complex business world, the relationships between companies can be equally complex. Thus, two companies could be customers of each other, as well as competitors in some contexts and potential partners in others. While marketing only deals with the customer relationship, business development can ferret out possibilities for co-operation in all the other areas, leading to the identification of a broader array of value creation opportunities and a much richer relationship.

Unfortunately, there is almost no literature on business development as a discipline. Academics have ignored this very important area where there is a strong need to understand, organize and codify the field to make a discipline out of it.

Business development has several interesting aspects, as set out below:

1   Taking a 'latent' business opportunity and making it 'manifest'. The objective is to get a high share of wallet, not just to capture low-hanging fruit. This requires that a company 'get in bed' with its customers at a high level: understand their strategic direction, become their trusted adviser (to such an extent that the company may even advise the customer not to purchase certain products from it).

2   Selling to a company in an integrated way. For example, since buying electricity has traditionally been highly decentralized by geography, BellSouth has many separate relationships with Georgia Power. The companies both have something to gain by integrating these many small transactions into an integrated relationship. They also have the potential to engage in reciprocal transactions by having BellSouth provide telecommunications services to Georgia Power throughout its market region.

3   Business development can mean getting into totally uncharted territory: for example, companies often follow their customers into new markets, such as foreign countries. (Some advertising agencies are currently following their large clients into emerging growth markets such as India and China.)

4   Partnering with a customer in order to create value for the customer's customers.

5   Business development can also mean co-operating with competitors. Often, companies find that they must co-opt their competitors in order to make a sale. This is quite common in defence contracting, where one competitor may be the prime contractor and another the subcontractor.

Emerging issues for customer-centred marketing

Several issues will have to be confronted as companies implement customer-centred marketing (see Figure 9.9):

1   Turf battles over the 'ownership' of a relationship. As cross-functional teams manage customer relationships, the issue of which functional area is the true 'owner' of the relationship may arise. Company executives must guard against this becoming a politically

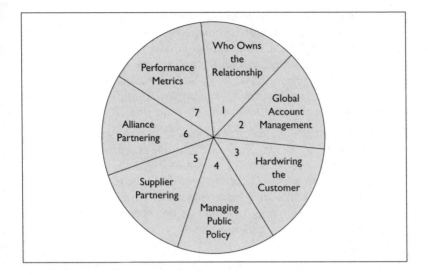

Figure 9.9 Emerging issues confronting customer-centred marketing

divisive force by aligning individual compensation systems with the achievement of corporate objectives, and by locating the ownership of relationships outside any functional area.

2   Global account management will become more of a trend as companies follow (or lead) their customers towards a global presence. This trend will receive added impetus as a result of rising economic integration and the evolution of the WTO (World Trade Organization).

3   Hardwiring the customer: this requires companies to achieve process-to-process integration across their boundaries. Inter-organizational strategies that leverage information technology capabilities are becoming more significant as a source of competitive advantage (Bensaou and Venkatraman, 1996). Customers and suppliers can benefit from entering into 'information partnerships' that help each to improve their business performance (Konsynski and McFarlan, 1990).

4   Managing public policy: since the successful practice of customer-centred marketing can result in individual companies achieving a very high share of the business, new types of anti-trust issue could arise. Firms must thus attempt to reshape public policy debate and educate policy-makers on the societal benefits of customer-centred marketing.

5   Supplier partnering: as discussed earlier, marketing will have to manage new types of suppliers, in addition to those that it has been accustomed to dealing with. As of now, it has few capabilities in this direction. In essence, marketing will create a network of inter-connected suppliers, all working for the benefit of the customer. Co-ordinating such a complex network requires that marketing create a clear blueprint for how it must function.

6   Alliance partnering: customer-centred marketing will also require marketers to engage in alliances with some competitors in order to serve their customers better. This can be a challenging juggling act, since the companies are likely to continue to be rivals in other are-nas. As mentioned earlier, marketing could learn some of the skills necessary by examining practices in defence contracting, where competitors routinely work together as prime and subcontractors.

7   Performance metrics: customer-centred marketing may die if there are no proper accounting/financial performance metrics, such as account-by-account revenue, inventory, cost analysis, P&L. Growth and profitability should be account by account. We currently do it by product portfolio but not by customer portfolio. Given that we are moving towards more fixed-cost marketing, this will require more frequent allocation of costs. This has to be done in a sophisticated and defensible way; typically, it means activity-based costing.

Conclusion and summary

When Theodore Levitt wrote about 'Marketing Myopia' over 40 years ago (Levitt, 1960), he catalysed a shift in marketing's perspective away from product features and towards customer needs. Over the succeeding decades, the marketing function gradually came to embrace a market orientation. However, for the sake of efficiency, the predominant focus remained on aggregations of customers rather than on individual cus-tomers (except in the case of business marketing). In this chapter, we have described how marketing will next evolve towards true customer-centredness, leveraging the technologies now available and affordable. Firms will discover that customer-centred marketing represents the most efficient use of their scarce resources and the best promise of superior financial returns. Making the shift to customer-centred marketing requires that firms make a number of significant changes to their culture, incentive systems and business processes.

Chapter
Drawing the strands together

philip j. kitchen

Aims

This chapter draws together the varied strands associated with the previous contributions. Inevitably, in an eclectic book of this type, not all of the critical issues connected with marketing have been, or can be, discussed; but the contributors have raised some vital aspects of marketing and its future which are worthy of consideration by practitioner and academic communities. Each contribution will be discussed in turn, and then a summary and conclusion will be offered.

It strikes me that marketing as a discipline is now standing at a crossroads. It is a powerfully representative way of expressing meaning about the exchange processes that take place in today's world. In these pages, each author has grappled with what marketing means from their own perspective. Perhaps that grappling process is going on now, within each reader, as you strive to understand what marketing was and is, what it has to contribute, and where it is going in the future. And we authors imagine that, in our own spatial and temporal space, we may have something worthwhile to say regarding its development and progression. Let us turn now to the contributors.

Chapter 2   Redesigning marketing to fit a different marketplace

Schultz, in his seminal work on marketing communications over many decades, has made many significant tangential contributions to the discipline of marketing. In Chapter 2 he has presented his thoughts almost as an artist paints a picture. In the background we have a representation of what marketing was; in the foreground we can see what marketing is now; and the picture is overlaid with a temporal and spatial view of what marketing is in process of becoming in the 21st century. In painting these word pictures, the value of marketing in theoretical and practical terms is enhanced and illuminated, but marketing has always been driven by the marketplace. Increasingly that *place* is becoming a *space* in which exchanges take place. Because of spatial changes, marketing must change as well. In all change scenarios there are bound to be disjunctions and discontinuities, so we find the old ways of creating exchanges co-existing alongside the new. But, just as production and sales orientations (ways of creating exchanges) are now fossilized in the sedimentary strata of marketing history, so the product-marketers and distribution-marketers, will tend to be similarly located as the customer-marketers adopt the high ground as personified by market, mind, and heart shares. The past may well be parent to the future, but the child needs to grow and change in differing contextual circumstances. Marketing itself, in the first century of its development, has to grow, flex and change. If anything, this ability is the hallmark of marketing. What a pity if the old adage rings true:

> The sermon had ended,
> The priest had descended;
> Delighted were they ...
> But they preferred the old way. (Anon.)

'The old way' is rapidly being supplanted by the need to practise marketing in multiple and simultaneous modalities and the need to move towards inbound rather than outbound flows of marketing. This second point is remarkable as it occurs after over four decades of development of the marketing concept which Levitt (1960) assured us was to be focused on the needs of buyers rather than sellers. It is evident, however, in many companies and nation-states that whatever marketing may be it is *not* necessarily always concerned with customer satisfactions, for too many enterprises dress organizationally-driven and profit-driven efficiencies up in the invisible clothing of consumer orientation. As a consequence, many consumers remain profoundly dissatisfied with their exchanges. The final point made by Schultz is the need for marketers to embrace and use financial models for marketing investments and returns:

In truth, customers are the true assets of organisations. The cash flows organisations generate are more critical to success than the tangible assets they control.

If we start to consider customers and the income flows they create as real organisational assets, we can start to treat them as assets in the same way tangible assets are valued and maintained. In other words, we would start to manage customers and customer income flows as assets *that have value and generate returns*. (Schultz and Kitchen, 2000; italics added)

And yet many organizations do not treat customers as assets. Often customers and their needs are not satisfied, *and no real attempt is being made to actually do this, save in a window-dressing form*. As a result, opportunities for building real relationships – *and I daresay, ongoing profitable interactions* – are forgone.

We can see that this picture of marketing as it was, is, and might yet be, has still to be developed fully. Perhaps readers may help in that developmental process?

Chapter 3   Rethinking the value concept in marketing

As in the previous section, van Raaij and Poiesz point to the diminishing effectiveness of traditional marketing tools, techniques and processes. To the authors, added value is the very essence of the marketing concept, and yet that concept is under constant pressure and criticism. The essence of the argument is that the old approach to added value (see Campo and Gilbrecht, 1999), comprising certain features (*ad hoc, unidimensional*, and *manufacturer defined*), has to be supplanted and replaced by the new: *long-term*, *multidimensional* and *consumer defined*.

As with Schultz's contribution in Chapter 2, this again suggests that there is something sadly awry in the state of marketing. Increasingly, products and services – in whatever form and wherever found – have to *be integrated* from a consumer/customer perspective. This supports the argument found in Schultz and Kitchen (2000, p. 62) that the final stage of integrated marketing communication is integrated marketing where financial and strategic balance is achieved. Total organizational value will and must be measured by the value *not only perceived but also received* by consumers.

Van Raaij and Poiesz, however, hesitate on the edge of predicting consumer behaviour in the future. There are strong market signals that marketing is moving from the mass to the micro, where more and more emphasis will be placed on building and maintaining relationships with individual consumers; facilitated, of course, by the infrastructural technology that allows these interactions to take place. The database of personalized information will act as a great facilitator in underpinning these relations.

There are, however, some points with which readers will take issue. Data gathering and knowledge extraction will probably increase in terms of organizational importance. Simultaneously, however, there may be a consumer backlash against various forms of marketing which are *ostensibly and overtly* organizationally oriented. For example, call centres seem to be one of the worst developments associated with the end of the 20th century and start of the 21st. Few, if any, call centres seem to have any idea of their sheer nuisance value. Readers will equally be unsure as to whether the number of brands will, in fact, be decreased markedly from *any* organization in a world where everything is branded. However, as van Riel and Berens indicate in Chapter 7, corporate brands as the nurturing protective device covering individual brands will become ever more important. Readers will need to be convinced, however, that marketing itself will be turned upside-down. A preferred term might be 'outside-in' marketing, rather than the current 'inside-out' version. Indeed, adoption of 'outside-in' may well seem as if initially marketing has been turned upside-down from an organizational context (see Chapter 9).

Chapter 4   Knowledge transfer through marketing textbooks: the Howard and Sheth buyer behaviour typology

The argument developed by Walter van Waterschoot and Els Gilbrecht is particularly appropriate for practitioners of marketing, while simultaneously shedding light on a difficult conceptual area – that of buyer behaviour – and having resonance for all other conceptual and practical areas of marketing which appear in textbooks. As others have argued, marketing knowledge cannot be constrained inside an intellectual academic domain; it has instead to be understood and applied within particular contextual circumstances.

One important method of transmitting knowledge is through the use of marketing textbooks. Typically, these are used in undergraduate and postgraduate courses and modules throughout the world. They also play a significant role in post-experience training and executive courses and seminars (or at least there is an assumption that learned textbooks do play a leading role in the transmission of knowledge with, of course, extensive forays as needed into the marketing journals for more in-depth analysis). As an aside, of course, most – if not all – marketing textbooks find diverse ways of communicating *the same information* inside the managerial school (see Sheth, Gardner and Garrett, 1988: see pp. 96–105, and Chapter 1 in this volume).

Waterschoot and Gilbrecht undertake a detailed analysis – through the extant subsequent literature – into the Howard and Sheth buyer behaviour typology. By means of a content analysis the authors identify that a problem exists, even with this dominant model, in terms of inaccurate and incomplete transfer of knowledge, with many textbooks subsequently distorting its contents, and often without any formal comparison with original sources.

By extension, therefore, it may well be the case that basic building blocks of marketing are not only being transferred too loosely, but they may also lack the necessary and detailed conceptual rigorous analysis that should accompany subsequent writings. However, most marketing textbooks are written from a generalistic perspective for *general consumption of marketing per se*. They are not written from a detailed analytical perspective.

Admittedly, the above point would be the anticipated norm. However, there is a problem with approximation, intuition and creativity in *adapting* current and past building blocks and that is referred to by Thomas as epistemopathology, a type of sickness with all the power attributed by Levitt (1960) four decades before to marketing myopia.

To avoid this type of sickness, and to strengthen the foundations of marketing in terms of basic building blocks, further detailed analysis is required; that analysis would be welcomed from either the commercial or the academic realm.

Chapter 5   Professionalism in marketing: an oxymoron?

Michael Thomas joins the authors of Chapters 2–4 in arguing that current views of the marketing profession are too constrained. The current focus on creating exchanges that satisfy individual and organizational objectives needs to be extended to a more societally-oriented approach focused on the welfare of society in a local, national, regional and even global sense. Thus, in his argument, he draws close to that deployed by van Riel and Berens (see Chapter 7), albeit from a radically different philosophical perspective. The current focus is freighted and weighted towards the accomplishment of organizational goals, but needs to be further extended towards stakeholder values rather than just shareholder returns. Whether, in today's profit-driven society, stakeholder values can rank alongside, or even above, shareholder returns is debatable. Further, in today's global marketplace there are huge and continuous social and economic inequalities. Rather than address such inequalities, global capitalism apparently thrives in this type of scenario which, if persisted in, may actually threaten damage to the fabric of social democracy. Education, not only of marketing professionals but of the entire range of managerial activities, would appear to be part of the answer. Serious questions as to *how* can this take place revolve around such issues as:

- social trusteeship
- mutual empowerment
- constituent practice
- epistemopathology
- reward systems in business practice
- democracy and capitalism

and these have all yet to be addressed. What Michael Thomas has done is raise a number of warning flags regarding areas which, in my view, need to be addressed.

Chapter 6   How clients can improve their advertising by improving their decision-making

After many decades of assuming that advertising is apparently integral and essential to the marketing communication activities of large firms, it is interesting to read a chapter which points out that:

- most advertising expenditure results in ineffective or weak advertising
- advertising is often mismanaged, and little serious time is devoted to it by management
- research outcomes are often far removed from evaluating a commercial's selling power
- judgemental engagement with company advertising often takes place at the lowest levels of managerial hierarchies
- the current trade-off between profit and advertising may be misplaced
- advertising is capable of having short-term, medium-term and long-term effects on consumer purchasing

John Philip Jones's proposed solutions to these endemic problems in advertising and its management are as set out below.

1   We need to measure behavioural effects of advertising as compared to the current measurement of attitudinal change. This will require, of course, programmed and specific solutions to current measurement approaches.

2   We need to return to higher levels of agency creativity, as compared to current starvation of agency renumeration (*and creativity*) via the fee-based system of compensation and reduced commissions.

3   There should be a concomitant acknowledgement of experimentation and greater quality control over advertising.

4   There must be reconsideration, or even outlawing, of company advertising policies (CAPs) which may be based on suppositions developed in earlier stages of economic and social development, not to mention company development.

Notably, this author also highlights the emergence of a consumer-empowered society and brand communications. He also highlights the need for more integrated approaches to communications and marketing, a point asserted by previous authors and echoed by those following.

Chapter 7   Corporate branding: the marketing perspective

CEOs under fire; plunging share prices; loss of shareholder confidence; sacking senior executives; revolving board room doors; failing to sell or tell convincing stories ... these are all illustrative of the need for chief executive officers, board level personnel, corporate communication directors, and the organisations they represent to *communicate effectively* with stakeholders who would impact on organisational performance. All are part and parcel of the fiercely competitive environment of the 21st century globalized marketplace. (Kitchen and Schultz, 2001, p. 3)

This quotation sounds like a familiar story as seen regularly in the pages of the *Financial Times, Wall Street Journal*, or any business magazine or periodical dealing with large firm reportage. Van Riel and Berens state that corporate branding has become much more important in recent decades. They cite three significant trends, as shown below, to which I add a fourth,

1   Increasing numbers of mergers and acquisitions.
2   Social responsibility and corporate openness.
3   The rising costs of advertising for individual product brands (see previous section) means that businesses can amortize costs by using a 'corporate umbrella' of one form or another. *And*
4   Consumers often make associations between individual brands they value, purchase, and are loyal to, and the corporate entity that owns and manages the brands. The following questions seem to crop up with alarming regularity:
    (a)   What does the corporation stand for?
    (b)   Which personalities are running the corporation?
    (c)   Is the firm a good corporate citizen?
    (d)   Can the business be seen to be socially responsible?

Of key concern to readers is the linkage between product evaluation and corporate brand associations. The evidence amassed by the contributors and in the previous work of van Riel indicate not only that such linkages do exist, but also that they are playing a significant role in purchase or non-purchase decisions. Thus, what seems initially to be part of the public affairs/public relations function, often divorced from marketing organizationally, may significantly impact bottom, middle and top line performance.

Chapter 8   Let's do the time warp again: a marketing manifesto for retro revolutionaries

Stephen Brown's ideas are now gaining wide acceptance on both sides of the Atlantic. In his chapter he discusses in some depth the various critiques that have been made of old-style marketing approaches, and his critique comprises both historical review and parlous practice. His five-step model resembles a line-dancing rhythm with various steps identified in history and practice:

Step1 Turn away
Step2 Look back
Step3 Move together
Step4 Hold tight
Step5 Repeat

Step 1 comprises both an attack on old-style marketing *and* a radical alternative, preferably with an appropriate new title (see the eight Es).

However, the outcome of 'turning away' means turning backwards, so that 2002 means revisiting 1968 with all its emphasis on old-style marketing. The new clothes may be nothing more than old clothes being remade and re-marketed.

Step 2, looking back, comprises re-inventing and re-investing, redeploying, re-broadcasting, resuscitating and repackaging, with retro systems being applied in many product and service areas. Meanwhile, recycling of old television programmes has done a great deal to encourage satellite and cable switching (perhaps a deliberate strategy by television companies as they splinter into myriads of channels). Retro has become a major part of the marketing game in the 21st century.

Step 3, move together, suggests that many retro marketing activities appeal to consumers' anti-marketing sentiments. In a world awash with commercialization, it is intriguing to think of companies and their brands as old-fashioned and responsive to an old-style scenario where 'the customer is always right'.

Step 4 suggests first that retro marketing, far from being new is, in fact, a well-observed historical phenomenon. Second, post-modernism contains many retrospective features which are integral to it; yet retro predates post-modernism. Both, however, are part of the same anti-establishment perspective. As Brown astutely observes, so much of *the new* inevitably means redevelopment of *the old*, which means – among other things – that product life cycles are cunningly (and perhaps invisibly) replaced by product life circles.

Finally, in *Step 5*, the dance continues. Despite marketing being attacked on all sides, from within and without, it is still very much alive. Despite business schools' incapacity to contain it fully, marketing is part of the street on which we all live, a point observed in our final contribution.

Chapter 9   The future of marketing

In this chapter, marketing turns full circle. In Chapter 2, Don Schultz argued specifically for consumer-centred marketing. Here, Sheth and Sisodia argue powerfully that the initial catalyst – namely a focus on customer needs – did succeed in moving marketing and marketers towards customer orientation. However, at that time, that focus was efficiency-based and resulted in customer aggregations rather than individual customers. By using technologies *now available and affordable*, businesses can now start to focus on individual customers (*pace* Levi Jeans available in made to measure). Such a customer-centred focus offers the most efficient use of scarce organizational resources and promises improved financial returns. But, as observed elsewhere (see Schultz and Kitchen, 2000), such focus does not just entail tinkering with promotional mix elements and dressing it up as relationship marketing. Instead, refocusing implies significant change in terms of organizational culture, reward systems and business process re-engineering.

Summary and conclusion

What this chapter has shown is that marketing – at least in its current taught and textual form, and probably within the managerial school – has encountered difficulties, doubts, criticisms and critiques, and these have all emerged (apparently) and gathered in intensity, in the last decade of the 20th century and the first few years of the 21st century. This is just one small period of time, but it is enough to radically re-shape how marketing is perceived and how it is practised. Albert Einstein commented: 'the significant problems we face cannot be solved at the same level of thinking we were at when we created them' (cited in Covey, 1989). I am unsure whether we have created problems in marketing. I am, however, convinced that old-style marketing dressed up in new streetwise clothing will not cut much ice in today's marketspaces. But Einstein's quote is relative. Taking its wisdom to heart offers opportunity for new ways of thinking which will result in new ways of theorizing, which in turn implies new ways of behaving. That is the opportunity and the challenge.

A meeting of minds

philip j. kitchen

Introduction

In the first chapter I promised readers that I 'would get out of the way' so that the contributors could 'speak for themselves'. Chapter 10 was an attempt to draw the strands together to provide an overview or synopsis of each chapter. Now, of course, it is my turn to make a few brief concluding comments which I hope will find resonance in the minds of readers. These comments are centred on just two questions.

1 Does marketing have a future?
2 Upon what criteria does that future depend?

Does marketing have a future?

The answer to this is both yes and no. No, I do not believe that marketing does have a future so long as it is straitjacketed in its oft-repeated rhetoric and dictums. Too many businesses and too many organizations have proclaimed allegiance to marketing and the marketing concept, yet what they offer to customers is, at best, marketing that is focused on scale efficiencies and competitive copying, while simultaneously dressing it up in a form of rhetoric that is:

(a) meant to be believed by customers and consumers
(b) intended to indicate a customer-orientation by the supplying organization

This time-honoured marketing approach, which I have described else-where *as a form of rhetoric* (see Kitchen, 2003), is frankly unattractive and unappealing both to practitioners and students of marketing. It is also a form of marketing that denigrates customers and consumers by *appearing to take their needs seriously*, but then continuing with *business as usual*.

However, the answer is also 'yes' for, as we have seen within the pages of this text, *marketing does have a future!* But, such a future is based on customer-centred marketing, which implies deep and expen-sive organizational restructuring to become customer-focused and customer-driven: a form of marketing described elsewhere as *the reality of marketing* (see Kitchen, 2003).

Now let me revert back to a quotation already given in Chapter 1 from Wroe Alderson where he stated:

> The best analogy for the capacity of a system to survive is the health of a biolog-ical organism ... it is rational to exercise proper care to keep the body or the sys-tem healthy. The prime strategy is a ... strategy of avoidance. The individual tries to avoid infection or other conditions that might cause illness. Through occa-sional medical examination he hopes for early detection of what might otherwise become an incurable and otherwise fatal disease. The executive watches for mal-adjustment in the system and attempts to provide proper remedies. Above all, he tries to prevent the system from falling into the condition that has been called the extinction mode. (Alderson, 1964)

In chiasmus pattern terms and based on the preceding chapters, the fol-lowing points can be made:

1 Marketing is not in an extinction mode, and all the evidence seems to point to this as unlikely in the next decade.

2 There are, however, maladjustments in the system, and these malad-justments need to be corrected by practitioners in terms of acting and behaving, and by theorists lest they be swallowed in the slough of oft-repeated dictums, which may not correspond to encountered realities from product and service providers and from public sector organizations.

3 This book, edited though it may be, is an attempt to provide proper remedies or an attempt to re-adjust the lens or microscope through which marketing can be seen more clearly.

4 Practitioners can see early medical examinations as regular attempts by theorists to examine and re-examine what marketing is, what it means, and how it might best be deployed.

5   Infection, in marketing's case, can be seen as delivery of accepted norms, creeds, models and processes, without any real attempt to critique inherent weaknesses.

6   I believe the prime strategy *not to be one of avoidance*, as this will no longer work. Plainly, marketing has entered a stage in terms of its disciplinary development that does appear to be a type of crisis, but it still has a contribution to make both in terms of potentiality and in actuality. Approaches have been made within the pages of this book as to what marketing's potential and actual contribution might be; but it will never be made, unless we tackle marketing at its roots instead of slashing wildly at the branches.

7   All the evidence seems to be that the system has the capacity to resist disease and to rise above entropy. But, again, *custodians must exercise proper care*. Custodianship extends well beyond supply-side considerations.

So, overall, marketing as a discipline, theory and practice does have a future.

Upon what criteria does that future depend?

The need (finally) to treat customers as assets

The driving force behind organizations has to become the customers: their needs, their wants, their desires. For far too long already, marketing has taken as a central tenet the need for organizations to become customer-focused and customer-driven, and yet, as we have seen in these pages, this has not really happened. Maybe the reason why it has not happened has to do with technology not keeping pace with ideas, concepts and philosophies. Today, however, that is no longer the case. Technology – in the form of individualized and personalized mechanisms of interfacing with people – is already here, but many companies are resisting this trend. The new wine of customer relationships simply will not fit into the bottles or containers of old-style marketing. The new wine (or new philosophies, approaches, or concepts) requires new bottles into which the wine can be poured, otherwise we are indeed toying with marketing that is increasingly sick.

The need to develop integrated marketing

There have been many books and articles espousing integrated market-ing, and its diversity of subfields. Integrated marketing means that *all* marketing activities, systems and processes have to be focused on creat-ing exchanges, *and not just satisfactory exchanges in the traditional mar-keting sense.* Instead of satisfying customers, organizations need to go the extra mile in delivering above the norm exchanges because, if they do what all other companies in the sector are doing, there is no scope for differential advantage. Instead, organizations need to *delight* customers through the multiple reference points by which the interface takes place.

The need to get beyond the idea that current textbooks deliver the essence of marketing

To be frank, there are no pat answers to marketing problems. Every mar-keting question, in every organization, needs to be determined according to an understanding of the dynamics of the served market (which may consist of many customers, each with individualized expectations), and as seen by a specific organization facing a specific market. Without this dual understanding, there is no rational basis for applying marketing. However, this understanding cannot be derived from a study of market-ing textbooks; instead, the books should serve as a starting point for a detailed data-driven exploration of what customers want, and how an organization can become customer-focused and customer-driven in order to deliver what is wanted. The focus and drive, needless to say, requires substantive organizational investment and restructuring. Adopting the philosophy of marketing is only a starting point.

The need to focus on stakeholders as well as shareholders

Shareholders, undoubtedly, will always be with us. Their needs are known and recognized. But, today, satisfying shareholders alone is insufficient. In 1990, Broom and Dozier commented: 'All business in a democratic soci-ety begins with public permission and exists by public approval' (p. xi).

I believe many organizations forget this principle at their peril. At the present time, we live in a society where capitalist democracy holds sway as the most appropriate paradigm by which people can live lives that are relatively free, and under which they can participate in democratic structures and make informed choices about purchase opportunities.

Ethics, and business ethics, can be determined by the dominant societal coalition at any specific point in time. Who is to say whether, looking back one hundred years from now in the 22nd century, whether many of the structures deemed necessary in our time will not then be seen as historical anachronisms? Stakeholder values are rapidly becoming more important in terms of what corporate entities actually do and, indeed, what they are allowed to do (genetically modified foods and Nike would seem to be current illustrative examples).

The need for promotional expenditure that is governed by creative content where outcomes are measured in behavioural terms

So much of promotional activity, as evidenced by its proliferation all around us – a sort of cultural background wallpaper – is essentially banal and uninteresting. The repeated shouting of discordant voices (albeit tempered by using the same hymn sheet in an integrated manner) has become a minor irritant to which we are all exposed on an ongoing basis, almost from cradle to grave. So much of it, though, is banal and uninteresting not only to consumers but also to the companies who develop it, and transmit it via multitudinous forms of media. A return to more (not less) creativity would doubtless be beneficial. Again, however, such creativity needs to be derived from an outside-in process, not the current inside-out approach. Behavioural measurement of promotional outcomes crops up again and again in the academic and practitioner literature, but it is a long way from being the norm. Maybe the time has now arrived when hierarchy of effects models, with all the attitudinal components contained therein, need to be supplanted and replaced by behaviourally-driven models related to return on investment (ROI) or return on customer investment (ROCI) criteria. Either way, a closer alliance between marketing and finance is required.

The need for corporations to take corporate branding more seriously

I am unsure about the words 'corporate branding'. In *The Corporate Umbrella* (see Kitchen and Schultz, 2001), we used the term (the umbrella concept) to mean the following:

1   It acts as a force-field metaphor, nurturing, protecting, and providing the resource-fertile environment to grow individual brands and

strategic business units, but it also builds and nurtures stakeholder relationships. Both are potentially irreplaceable assets.

2   It acts as a metaphor in the way it can be operationalized at the corporate level. In other, integrated communication it acts like the ribs of an umbrella in that the various communication activities (including marketing) of the corporation support the overall communication system. Mismanage or lose one of the communication 'ribs' (such as corporate citizenship, crisis management, social responsibility, or public affairs) and the whole communication coverage of the organization becomes unstable and exposed to the stormy winds of external forces.

Yet many corporations – while apparently proclaiming that their existence relies solely on satisfying customers and consumers – more overtly satisfy senior management teams (especially CEOs) first of all, and then their shareholders. Even today we have the amazing spectacle of loss-making corporate entities continuing to reward senior staff with huge pay rises, bonuses and stock options, while customers are still expected to buy, and shareholders to 'go with the flow' or with current management practices. Moreover, in the global market of today, there are few if any restraining mechanisms to control multinational and global corporations in terms of encouraging compliance with socially responsible practices. It strikes me that most global businesses will not comply while there is no global force capable of legislating in favour of consumers and stakeholders.

Towards a conclusion

The final need is that marketing itself go beyond re-packaging or producing 'new improved versions of'

Admittedly, marketing is now under the microscopic scrutiny of many stakeholders. I believe that much of that scrutiny has not yet been engaged in by those assigned to deliver the disciplinary tenets. By that, I mean delivery of the standardized norms of marketing as in training courses, and undergraduate and postgraduate training. Maybe there is insufficient time? Maybe the tenets are so well grounded that they cannot be challenged? Maybe the dominance of the American model of marketing is so well entrenched that all future writers can do is produce watered-down versions or adaptations of the dominant approach?

I believe readers will find the time, however. Seek to challenge the accepted (if, in fact, it is accepted). Tackle the models, techniques, processes and systems to see if they really hold water in the harsh competitive realities of the 21st century.

Maybe the task of marketing intellectuals in the next few years of the 21st century is to grapple with some of the issues raised within this book. Certainly, the classroom or the lecture theatre is an ideal training ground in which questions can be raised, though I suspect that most answers will be forged in the crucible of critical discussion and marketplace practice.

In closing, let me paraphrase a statement from Stephen Hawking: 'If we do discover a broad theory, it should in time be understandable by everyone, not just a few scientists [marketing theorists]. Then we shall all, philosophers, scientists, and just ordinary people, be able to take part in the discussion of the question' (paraphrased from Hawking, 1992). His question admittedly deals with why humans and the universe exist. Our humbler questions are inherently to do with the theory and practice of marketing. Our exploration, albeit on a lesser scale, will do much to improve the quality of human life (as consumers) on this planet. Let us enjoy the journey and the exploration.

References

Aaker, D.A. (1996) *Building Strong Brands*, The Free Press, New York.

Aaker, D.A. and Keller, K.L. (1990) 'Consumer evaluations of brand extensions', *Journal of Marketing*, 54, 1, pp. 27–41.

Alderson, W. (1957) *Marketing Behavior and Executive Action*, Richard D. Irwin, Homewood, IL.

Alderson, W. (1964) cited in R. Cox, W. Alderson and S. Shapiro (eds) (1964), *Theory in Marketing*, Richard D. Irwin, Homewood, IL, p. 101.

Alderson, W. (1965) *Dynamic Marketing Behavior*, Richard D. Irwin, Homewood, IL.

Alderson, W. and Green, P. (1964) *Planning and Problem Solving in Marketing*, Richard D. Irwin, Homewood, IL.

Arndt, J. (1976) 'The Marketing Thinking of Tomorrow: Beyond the Marketing Concept Toward New Dignity and Responsible Freedom for Managers and Consumers', *Working Paper*, Norwegian School of Economics and Business Administration, February.

Ascherson, N. (1999) 'The Indispensable Englishman', *New Statesman*, 29 January, p. 26.

Assael, H. (1985) *Marketing Management: Strategy and Action*, Kent Publishing Company, Boston, MA.

Assael, H. (1992) *Consumer Behavior and Marketing Action*, 4th edn, Kent Publishing Company, Boston, MA.

Baker, M. (ed.) (1999a) *Encyclopaedia of Marketing*, International Thomson Press, London.

Baker, M. (1999b) 'The Future of Marketing', in Baker (1999a), pp. 816–31.

Bartels, R. (1962) *The Development of Marketing Thought*, Richard D. Irwin, Homewood, IL.

Bartels, R. (1983) 'Is Marketing Defaulting Its Responsibilities?', *Journal of Marketing*, 38 (October).

Barzun, J. (2000) *From Dawn to Decadence. 500 Years of Western Cultural Life: 1500 to the Present*, HarperCollins, New York.

Baudrillard, J. (1994) *The Illusion of the End*, trans. C. Turner, Polity, Cambridge.

Bearden, W.O., Ingram, T.N. and La Forge, R.W. (1995) *Marketing: Principles and Perspectives*, Irwin, Chicago, IL.

Belk, R. (2001) 'Unpacking My Library: The Marketing Professor in the Age of Electronic Reproduction', *Journal of Marketing*, 66, 1, pp. 47–8.

Benjamin, W. (1999) *The Arcades Project*, trans. H. Eiland and K. McLaughlin, Belknap, Cambridge, MA.

Bensaou, M. and Venkatraman, N. (1996) 'Inter-Organizational Relationships and Information Technology: A Conceptual Synthesis and a Research Framework', *European Journal of Information Systems*, 5, 2, pp. 84–91.

Berens, G., van Riel, C.B.M. and van Bruggen, G.H. (2002) 'The added value of corporate brands: When do organizational associations affect product evaluations?', Unpublished manuscript, Erasmus University, Rotterdam.

Bettman, J.R. (1979) *An Information Processing Theory of Consumer Choice*, Addison-Wesley, Reading, MA.

Bircham, E. and Charlton, J. (2001) *Anti-Capitalism: A Guide to the Movement*, Bookmarks, London.

Bogart, M.H. (1995) *Artists, Advertising and the Borders of Art*, University of Chicago Press, Chicago, IL.

Bové, J. and Dufour, F. (2001) *The World is Not for Sale: Farmers Against Junk Food*, Verso, London.

Bovée, C.L., Houston, M.J. and Thill, J.V. (1995) *Marketing*, McGraw-Hill, New York.

Brassington, F.L. and Pettitt, S. (1997) *Principles of Marketing*, Pitman, London.

Briggs, A. and Snowman, D. (1996) *Fins de Siècle: How Centuries End*, Yale University Press, New Haven, CT.

Broom, G.M. and Dozier, D.M. (1990) *Using Research in Public Relations: Applications to Program Management*, Prentice-Hall, London.

Brown, S. (1995) *Postmodern Marketing*, Routledge, London.

Brown, S. (1998) *Postmodern Marketing Two: Telling Tales*, International Thomson Press, London.

Brown, S. (1999) 'Millennial Madness, *fin de siècle* Fever and the End of the End of Marketing', in S. Brown and A. Patterson (eds), *Proceedings of the Marketing Paradiso Conclave*, University of Ulster, Belfast, pp. 1–13.

Brown, S. (2001a) *Marketing – The Retro Revolution*, Sage, London.

Brown, S. (2001b) 'The Retromarketing Revolution', *International Journal of Management Reviews*, 3, 4, pp. 303–20.

Brown, S. (2001c) 'Torment Your Customers (They'll Love It)', *Harvard Business Review*, 79, 9, pp. 82–8.

Brown, S. (2002) 'Reading Wroe: On the Biopoetics of Alderson's Functionalism', unpublished paper.

Brown, S. and Patterson, A. (2000) *Imagining Marketing: Art, Aesthetics and the Avant-Garde*, Routledge, London.

Brown, T.J. (1998) 'Corporate associations in marketing: Antecedents and consequences', *Corporate Reputation Review*, 1, 3, pp. 215–33.

Brown, T.J. and Dacin, P.A. (1997) 'The company and the product: Corporate associations and consumer product responses', *Journal of Marketing*, 61, 1, pp. 68–84.

Bryman, A. (1995) *Disney and his Worlds*, Routledge, London.

Buck-Morss, S. (1991) *The Dialectics of Seeing: Walter Benjamin and the Arcades Project*, MIT Press, Cambridge, MA.

Bull, M. (1995) 'On Making Ends Meet', in M. Bull (ed.), *Apocalypse Theory and the Ends of the World*, Blackwell, Oxford, pp. 1–17.

Butler, D. *et al.* (1999) 'Cover Story: Attention All Shoppers', *Time*, 2 August, pp. 38–43.

Butscher, S.A. (2002) *Customer Loyalty Programmes and Clubs*, 2nd edn, Gower, Aldershot.

Cairncross, F. (1997) *The Death of Distance*, HBS Press, Boston, MA.

Campo, K. and Gilbrecht, E. (1999) 'Branding and Brand Management', in M.T. Baker (ed.), *Encyclopedia of Marketing*, International Thomson Business Press, London, pp. 376–89.

Carey, N. (1999) *The Faber Book of Utopias*, Faber & Faber, London.

Carlin, G. (1997) *Brain Droppings*, Hyperion, New York.

Cockburn, A., St. Clair, J. and Sekula, A. (2000) *Five Days That Shook the World: Seattle and After*, Verso, London.

Cohen, B. and Greenfield, J. (1997) *Ben & Jerry's Double Dip: How to Run a Values-Led Business and Make Money, Too*, Fireside, New York.

Cohen, R. (1963) 'The measurement of corporate images', in John W. Riley (ed.), *The Corporation and its Publics*, John Wiley, New York and London, pp. 48–63.

Colley, R.H. (1961) *Defining Advertising Goals for Measured Advertising Results*, The Association of National Advertisers, New York

Cook, J.W. (2001) *The Arts of Deception: Playing With Fraud in the Age of Barnum*, Harvard University Press, Cambridge, MA.

Cooper, R.G. (1998) *Product Leadership: Creating and Launching Superior New Products*, Perseus Books, New York.

Covey, S.R. (1989) *The Seven Habits of Highly Effective People*, Simon & Schuster, New York, p. 42.

Cox, R., Alderson, W. and Shapiro, S. (eds) (1964) *Theory in Marketing*, Richard D. Irwin, Homewood, IL.

Cravens, D.W., Hills, G.E. and Woodruff, R.B. (1980) *Marketing Decision Making: Concepts and Strategy*, revised edn, Irwin, Homewood, IL.

Dacin, P.A. and Smith, D.C. (1994) 'The effect of brand portfolio characteristics on consumer evaluations of brand extensions', *Journal of Marketing Research*, 31 (May), pp. 229–42.

Davis, S. and Meyer, C. (1998) *Blur. The Speed of Change in the Connected Economy*, Warner Books, New York.

Day, G.S. and Montgomery, D.B. (1999) 'Charting new directions for marketing', *Journal of Marketing*, 63, 1, pp. 3–13.

Day, G.S. and Wensley, R. (1983) 'Marketing Theory with a Strategic Orientation', *Journal of Marketing*, 47 (Fall), pp. 101–10.

Dholakia, N. and Arndt, J. (eds) (1985) *Changing the Course of Marketing: Alternative Paradigms for Widening Marketing Theory*, JAI Press, Greenwich, CT.

Dibb, S., Simkin, L., Pride, W.M. and Ferrell, O.C. (1994) *Marketing Concepts and Strategies*, 2nd European edn, Houghton Mifflin, London.

Dickinson, P. and Svensen, N. (2000) *Beautiful Corporations: Corporate Style in Action*, Pearson, London.

Doyle, P. (1994) *Marketing Management and Strategy*, Prentice-Hall, New York.

Duncan, T. (2001) *IMC: Using Advertising and Promotion to Build Brands*, Irwin/McGraw-Hill, Boston, MA.

Engel, J.F., Blackwell, R.D. and Miniard, P.W. (1986) *Consumer Behaviour*, 5th edn, The Dryden Press, Chicago, IL.

Firat, A.F., Dholakia, N. and Bagozzi, R.P. (eds) (1987) *Philosophical and Radical Thought in Marketing*, Lexington Books, Lexington, MA.

Fombrun, C.J., Gardberg, N.A. and Sever, J.M. (2000) 'The Reputation Quotient: A multi-stakeholder measure of corporate reputation', *Journal of Brand Management*, 7, 4, pp. 241–55.

Frank, T. (2000) *One Market Under God: Extreme Capitalism, Market Populism and the End of Economic Democracy*, Doubleday, New York.

Franklin, A. (2002) 'Consuming Design, Consuming Retro', in S. Miles *et al.* (eds), *The Changing Consumer: Markets and Meanings*, Routledge, London, pp. 90–103.

Frum, D. (2000) *How We Got Here. The 70s: The Decade that Brought you Modern Life – For Better or Worse*, Basic Books, New York.

Fullerton, R. (1987) 'The Poverty of Ahistorical Analysis: Present Weakness and Future Cure in U.S. Marketing Thought', in Firat, Dholakia and Bagozzi (1987).

Gilmore, J.H. and Pine II, B.J. (1997) 'The Four Faces of Mass Customization', *Harvard Business Review*, 75, 1 (January–February), pp. 91–101.

Godin, S. (2000) *Unleashing the Ideavirus, Do You Zoom*, Dobbs Ferry, New York.

Goulding, C. (2002) 'Corsets, Silk Stockings and Evening Suits: Retro Shops and Retro Junkies', in S. Brown and J.F. Sherry, Jr (eds), *Time, Space, and the Market: Ecumenical Essays on the Rise of Retroscapes*, M.E. Sharpe, New York, in press.

Grant, J. (1999) *The New Marketing Manifesto*, Orion, London.

Guiltinan, J.P. and Paul, G.W. (1994) *Marketing Management: Strategies and Programs*, international edn/5th edn, McGraw-Hill, New York.

Handelman, J.M. and Arnold, S.J. (1999) 'The role of marketing actions with a social dimension: Appeals to the institutional environment', *Journal of Marketing*, 63, 3, pp. 33–48.

Handy, C. (1995) *The Empty Raincoat*, Arrow Books, London (first published by Hutchinson, London, in 1994).

Harris, D. (2000) *Cute, Quaint, Hungry and Romantic: The Aesthetics of Consumerism*, Basic Books, New York.

Hawking, S. (ed.) (1992) *Stephen Hawking's A Brief History of Time: A Reader's Companion*, Bantam Press, London, p. 175.

Hawkins, D.I., Best, R.J. and Coney, K.A. (1992) *Consumer Behaviour. Implications for Marketing Strategy*, 5th edn, Irwin, Homewood, IL.

Hedberg, A. and Singh, S. (2001) 'Retro Chic or Cheap Relics?', *Marketing Week*, 18 (October), pp. 24–7.

Heeringa, V. (1998) 'Of Ad Agency Commissions, An Ad-hating Elite, Et Cetera', *Independent Business Weekly*, 25 March, p. 23.

Heilbrunn, B. (1998) 'In Search of the Lost Aura: The Object in the Age of Marketing Romanticism', in S. Brown *et al.* (eds), *Romancing the Market*, Routledge, London, pp. 187–201.

Hertz, N. (2001) *The Silent Takeover: Global Capitalism and the Death of Democracy*, Heinemann, London.

Hewison, R. (1987) *The Heritage Industry: Britain in a Climate of Decline*, Methuen, London.

Hine, T. (1995) *The Total Package: The Secret History and Hidden Meanings of Boxes, Bottles, Cans and Other Persuasive Containers*, Back Bay Books, Boston, MA.

Holbrook, M.B. (2001) 'Wroe Alderson (1957) *Marketing Behavior and Executive Action*', *ACR News*, Winter, pp. 37–8.

Holbrook, M.B. and Schindler, R.M. (1994) 'Age, Sex and Attitude Toward the Past as Predictors of Consumers' Aesthetic Tastes for Cultural Products', *Journal of Marketing Research*, 31 (August), pp. 412–22.

Holbrook, M.B. and Schindler, R.M. (1996) 'Market Segmentation Based on Age and Attitude Toward the Past: Concepts, Methods and Findings Concerning Nostalgic Influences on Consumer Tastes', *Journal of Business Research*, 37 (June), pp. 27–39.

Hollander, S.C. and Singh, A.K. (1994) 'Consumerism Revisited', in J.B. Schmitt *et al.* (eds), *Contemporary Marketing History*, Michigan State University, Ann Arbor, pp. 135–51.

Holt, D.B. (2002) 'Why do brands cause trouble? A dialectical theory of consumer culture and branding', *Journal of Consumer Research*, 29, 1 [forthcoming].

Hornby, A.S. (1989) *Oxford Advanced Learner's Dictionary of Current English*, 4th edn, Oxford University Press.

Horton, R.L. (1984) *Buyer Behaviour. A Decision-Making Approach*, Charles E. Merrill, Columbus, OH.

Howard, J.A. (1963) *Marketing Management: Analysis and Planning*, revised edn, Irwin, Homewood, IL.

Howard, J.A. (1974) 'The Structure of Buying Behaviour', in J.U. Farley, J.A. Howard and L. Winston Ring (eds), *Consumer Behaviour. Theory and Application*, Allyn & Bacon, Boston, MA.

Howard, J.A. (1977) *Consumer Behaviour: Application of Theory*, McGraw-Hill, New York.

Howard, J.A. (1989) *Consumer Behaviour in Marketing Strategy*, Prentice-Hall, Englewood Cliffs, NJ.

Howard, J. and Sheth, J.N. (1967) 'A Theory of Buyer Behaviour', in Reed Moyer (ed.), *Changing Marketing Systems Consumer, Corporate and Government Interfaces: Proceedings of the 1967 Winter Conference of the American Marketing Association*.

Howard, J. and Sheth, J.N. (1969) *The Theory of Buyer Behaviour*, John Wiley, New York.

Hunt, S.D. (1983) 'General Theories and Fundamental Explanada of Marketing', *Journal of Marketing*, 47 (Fall), pp. 9–17.

Hunt, S.D. (1989) 'Reification and Realism in Marketing', *Journal of Macromarketing*, 9 (Fall).

Hunt, S.D. (1991) *Modern Marketing Theory: Critical Issues in the Philosophy of Marketing Science*, Southwestern, Cincinnati.

Hunt, S.D. (1992) 'Marketing is ... ' *Journal of the Academy of Marketing Science*, 20, 4, pp. 301–11.

Jobber, D. (1995) *Principles and Practice of Marketing*, McGraw-Hill, London.

Jones, J.P. (1990) 'The Double Jeopardy of Sales Promotion', *Harvard Business Review*, 68, 5, pp. 145–52.

Jones, J.P. (2000) 'Advertising: The Cinderella of Business', *Market Leader*, 9, the World Advertising Research Center.

Kassarjian, H. (1977) 'Content Analysis in Consumer Research: Issues and Outlook', *Journal of Consumer Research*, 4 (June), pp. 8–18.

Kassarjian, H. and Healy, J.S. (1983) 'Advertising Substantiation and Advertising Response: A Content Analysis of Magazine Advertisements', *Journal of Marketing*, 47 (Winter), pp. 107–17.

Keller, K.L. (1993) 'Conceptualizing, measuring, and managing customer-based brand equity', *Journal of Marketing*, 57, 1, pp. 1–22.

Keller, K.L. and Aaker, D.A. (1998) 'The impact of corporate marketing on a company's brand extensions', *Corporate Reputation Review*, 1, 4, pp. 356–78.

Kinnear, T.C. and Bernhardt, K.L. (1986) *Principles of Marketing*, 2nd edn, Scott, Foresman, Glenview, IL.

Kitchen, P.J. (ed.) (2003) *The Rhetoric and Reality of Marketing: An International Managerial Approach*, Palgrave, Basingstoke (in press).

Kitchen, P.J. and Schultz, D.E. (eds) (2001) *Raising the Corporate Umbrella: Corporate Communications in the 21st Century*, Palgrave, Basingstoke.

Klein, N. (1999) *No Logo: No Space, No Choice, No Jobs: Taking Aim at the Brand Bullies*, Picador, New York.

Klein, N. (2000) *No Logo*, Flamingo, London.

Klein, N. (2000) *No Logo: Taking Aim at the Brand Bullies*, HarperCollins, London.

Konsynski, B.R. and McFarlan, F.W. (1990) 'Information Partnerships – Shared Data, Shared Scale', *Harvard Business Review*, 68, 5 (September/October), pp. 114–20.

Kotler, P. (1999) *Kotler on Marketing: How to Create, Win and Dominate Markets*, Free Press, New York.

Kotler, P. (2000) *Marketing Management: The Millennium Edition*, Prentice-Hall, Englewood Cliffs, NJ.

Kuhn, T.S. (1970) *The Structure of Scientific Revolutions*, University of Chicago Press, Chicago, IL.

Laird, P.W. (1998) *Advertising Progress: American Business and the Rise of Consumer Marketing*, Johns Hopkins University Press, Baltimore, MD.

Lakatos, I. (1968) 'Criticism and the methodology of scientific research programmes', *Proceedings of the Aristotelian Society*, 69, pp. 149–86.

Lavidge, R.F. and Steiner, G.A. (1961) 'A Model for Predictive Measurements of Advertising Effectiveness', *Journal of Marketing*, October, p. 61.

Lawson, H. (1998) 'Globalisation and the Social Responsibilities of Citizen-Professionals', AISED Conference, New York.

Lawson, R.W. (1995) 'Consumer behaviour', in Michael J. Baker (ed.), *Encyclopedia of Marketing*, Routledge, London.

Leach, W. (1993) *Land of Desire: Merchants, Power and the Rise of a New American Culture*, Pantheon, New York.

Lears, J. (1994) *Fables of Abundance: A Cultural History of Advertising in America*, Basic Books, New York.

Leeflang, P.S.H. (2001) 'The future of "marketing" is …', in S. Dibb, L. Simkin, W.M. Pride and O.C. Ferrell (eds), *Marketing: Concepts and Strategies*, Houghton Mifflin, Boston, MA, pp. 791–2.

Lehmann, U. (2000) *Tigersprung: Fashion in Modernity*, MIT Press, Cambridge, MA.

Levitt, T. (1960) 'Marketing Myopia', *Harvard Business Review*, 38, 4 (July/August), pp. 45–56.

Levitt, T. (1983) 'The Globalisation of Markets', *Harvard Business Review*, May–June, pp. 92–102.

Lindbloom, C. (1990) *Inquiry and Change: The Troubled Attempt to Understand and Shape Society*, Yale University Press, New Haven, CT.

Locke, C. (2001) *Gonzo Marketing: Winning Through Worst Practices*, Capstone, Oxford.

Lunn, J.A. (1974) 'Consumer Decision. Process Models', in Jagdish N. Sheth (ed.), *Models of Buying Behaviour. Conceptual, Quantitative and Empirical*, Harper & Row, New York.

Lusch, R.F. and Lusch, V.N. (1987) *Principles of Marketing*, Kent, Boston, MA.

Maathuis, O.J.M. (1999) 'Corporate branding: The value of the corporate brand to customers and managers', Unpublished doctoral dissertation, Erasmus University, Rotterdam.

McCarthy, E.J. and Perreault, W.D. (1993) *Basic Marketing*, 11th edn, Irwin, Homewood, IL.

McCarthy, J. (1960) *Basic Marketing: A Managerial Approach*, Irwin, Homewood, IL.

McDaniel, C. Jr (1982) *Marketing*, 2nd edn, Harper & Row, New York.

McDonald, M.H.B., De Chernatony, L. and Harris, F. (2001) 'Corporate marketing and service brands: Moving beyond the fast-moving consumer goods model', *European Journal of Marketing*, 35, 3/4, pp. 335–52.

McKendrick, N. (1982) 'Josiah Wedgwood and the Commercialisation of the Potteries', in N. McKendrick, J. Brewer and J.H. Plumb (eds), *Birth of a Consumer Society*, Europa, London, pp. 100–45.

McKenna, R. (1991) *Relationship Marketing*, Addison-Wesley, Reading, MA.

Maignan, I. and Ralston, D.A. (in press) 'Corporate social responsibility in Europe and the U.S.: Insights from businesses' self-presentations', *Journal of International Business Studies*.

Marchand, R. (1985) *Advertising the American Dream: Making Way for Modernity, 1920–1940*, University of California Press, Berkeley, CA.

Markin, R. (1982) *Marketing. Strategy and Management*, 2nd edn, Wiley, New York.

Mittal, B. and Sheth, J.N. (2001) *ValueSpace*, McGraw-Hill, New York.

Mitchell, A. (2001) 'Have Marketers Missed the Point of Marketing?', *Marketing Week*, 27 September.

Moore, R.L. (1994) *Selling God: American Religion in the Marketplace of Culture*, Oxford University Press.

Monbiot, G. (2000) *Captive State: The Corporate Takeover of Britain*, Palgrave, Basingstoke.

Oliver, G. (1986) *Marketing Today*, 2nd edn, Prentice-Hall International, London.

Parsons, A.J. (1996) 'Nestlé: The visions of local managers', *McKinsey Quarterly*, 2, pp. 4–29.

Peppers, D. and Rogers, M. (1993) *The One to One Future: Building Relationships One Customer at a Time*, Doubleday, New York.

Peppers, D., Rogers, M. and Dorf, B. (1999) 'Manager's Tool Kit: Is your Company Ready for One-to-One Marketing?', *Harvard Business Review*, 77, 1 (January–February), pp. 151–61.

Perkin, H. (1996) *The Third Revolution: Professional Elites in the Modern World*, Routledge, London.

Peter, P.J. and Olson, J.C. (1987) *Consumer Behaviour: Marketing Strategy Perspective*, Richard D. Irwin, Homewood, IL.

Peter, P.J. and Olson, J.C. (1994) *Understanding Consumer Behaviour*, Irwin, Homewood, IL.

Piercy, N. (2002) *Market-Led Strategic Change*, 3rd edn, Butterworth-Heinemann, Oxford.

Pine II, B.J. and Gilmore, J.H. (1999) *The Experience Economy*, Harvard Business School Press, Boston, MA.

Pine II, B.J., Victor, B. and Boyton, A.C. (1993) 'Making Mass Customization Work', *Harvard Business Review*, 71, 5 (September–October), pp. 91–103.

Poiesz, T.B.C. and van Raaij, W.F. (2002) *Synergetische Marketing. Een Visie op Oorzaken en Gevolgen van Veranderend Consumentengedrag (Synergetical Marketing. A Vision on Causes and Effects of Changing Consumer Behaviour)*, Financial Times/Pearson, Amsterdam.

Pride, W.H. and Ferrell, O.C. (1983) *Marketing*, 3rd edn, Houghton Mifflin, Boston, MA.

Pride, W.H. and Ferrell, O.C. (1991) *Marketing Concepts and Strategies*, 7th edn, Houghton Mifflin, Boston, MA.

Rewoldt, S.H., Scott, J.D. and Warshaw, M.R. (1981) *Introduction to Marketing Management*, 4th edn, Irwin, Homewood, IL.

Porter, M.E. (1985) *Competitive Advantage: Creating and Sustaining Superior Performance*, Free Press, New York.

Reynolds, T.J. and Gutman, J. (1984) 'Advertising is image management', *Journal of Advertising Research*, 24, 1, pp. 27–36.

Robinson, J. (1998) *The Manipulators: A Conspiracy to Make Us Buy*, Simon & Schuster, London.

Roddick, A. (2001) *Business as Unusual: The Triumph of Anita Roddick*, Thorsons, London.

Rokeach, M. (1973) *The Nature of Human Values*, The Free Press, New York.

Rosen, E. (2000) *The Anatomy of Buzz*, HarperCollins, London.

Runyon, K.E. (1977) *Consumer Behaviour and the Practice of Marketing*, Charles E. Merrill, Columbus, OH.

Rushkoff, D. (1999) *Coercion: The Persuasion Professionals and Why We Listen to What They Say*, Little, Brown, London.

Samuel, R. (1994) *Theatres of Memory Volume I: Past and Present in Contemporary Culture*, Verso, London.

Sawhney, M.S. and Kotler, P. (1999) 'Marketing in an Age of Information Democracy', Working Paper, Kellogg.

Schiffman, L.G. and Kanuk, L.K. (1994) *Consumer Behaviour*, 3rd edn, Prentice-Hall International, London.

Schmitt, B. (1999) *Experential Marketing*, Free Press, New York.

Schoell, W.F. and Guiltinan, J.P. (1995) *Marketing*, Prentice-Hall, Englewood Cliffs, NJ.

Schramm, W. and Roberts, D. (eds) (1971) *The Process and Effects of Mass Communication*, University of Illinois Press, Urbana, IL.

Schultz, D.E. and Kitchen, P.J. (2000) *Communicating Globally: An Integrated Marketing Approach*, NTC Business, Chicago, and Palgrave, Basingstoke, p. 187.

Schultz, D.E. and Walters, J.F. (1997) *Measuring Brand Communication ROI*, Association of National Advertisers, New York.

Schwartz, S.H. and Bilsky, W. (1987) 'Toward a universal psychological structure of human values', *Journal of Personality and Social Psychology*, 53, 3, pp. 550–62.

Schwartz, S.H. and Bilsky, W. (1990) 'Toward a theory of the universal content and structure of values: Extensions and cross-cultural replications', *Journal of Personality and Social Psychology*, 58, 5, pp. 878–91.

Scott, M.C. (1998) *Value Drivers*, John Wiley, Chichester.

Senge, P. (1994) *The Fifth Discipline Field Book*, Doubleday, New York.

Shapiro, S. and Walle, A.H. (eds) (1987) *Marketing: A Return to the Broader Dimensions*, American Marketing Association, Chicago, IL.

Sherry, J.F., Jr (1998) *Servicescapes: The Concept of Place in Contemporary Markets*, NTC Books, Chicago, IL.

Sheth, J.N. and Mittal, B. (1996) 'A Framework for Managing Customer Expectations', *Journal of Market Focused Management*, 1, 1, pp. 137–58.

Sheth, J.N. and Sisodia, R.S. (1995) 'Feeling the Heat: Making Marketing More Productive', *Marketing Management*, 4, 2, pp. 8–23.

Sheth, J.N. and Sisodia, S. (1997) 'Consumer behavior in the future', in R.A. Peterson (ed.), *Electronic Marketing and the Consumer*, Sage, Thousand Oaks.

Sheth, J.N. and Sisodia, R.S. (1999) 'Revisiting Marketing's Lawlike Generalizations', *Journal of the Academy of Marketing Science*, 27, 1, pp. 71–87.

Sheth, J.N. and Sisodia, R.S. (2000) 'Marketing's Final Frontier: The Automation of Consumption', in *Defying the Limits: Reaching New Heights in Customer Relationship Management*, Montgomery Research and Andersen Consulting, New York.

Sheth, G., Gardner, D.M. and Garrett, D.E. (1988) *Marketing Theory: Evolution and Evaluation*, John Wiley, New York.

Sheth, J.N., Sisodia, R.S. and Sharma, A. (2000) 'The Antecedents and Consequences of Customer-Centric Marketing', *Journal of the Academy of Marketing Science*, 28, 1, pp. 55–66.

Sivulka, J. (1998) *Soap, Sex and Cigarettes: A Cultural History of American Advertising*, Wadsworth, Belmont, CA.

Solomon, M.R. (1994) *Consumer Behaviour*, 2nd edn, Allyn & Bacon, Boston, MA.

Stern, B.B. (1992) 'Historical and Personal Nostalgia in Advertising Text: The *fin de siècle* Effect', *Journal of Advertising*, 21, 4, pp. 11–22.

Sung, J. and Tkaczyk, C. (2002) 'Who's on top and who flopped', *Fortune*, 145, 5, pp. 75–82.

Tarpey, L.X., Donnelly, J.H. Jr and Peter, J.P. (1979) *A Preface to Marketing Management*, Business Publications, Dallas, TX.

Thomas, M.J. (1996) 'The changing nature of the marketing profession and its requirements in marketing education', in S.A. Shaw and N. Hood (eds), *Marketing in Evolution,* Macmillan, London, pp. 190–205.

Thomas, M.J. (2002) 'Thoughts on building a just, market society', *Journal of Public Affairs*, 2, 2 [forthcoming].

Uncut (2001) 'There's a Riot Goin' On', *Uncut*, 44 (January), p. 46.

van Raaij, W.F. (1985) 'The psychological foundation of economics: the history of consumer theory', in C.T. Tan and J.N. Sheth (eds), *Historical Perspective in Consumer Research: National and International Perspectives*, National University of Singapore, pp. 8–13.

van Riel, C.B.M. (1995) *Principles of Corporate Communication*, Prentice-Hall, London.

Weinreich, L. (1999) *Eleven Steps to Brand Heaven: The Ultimate Guide to Buying an Advertising Campaign*, Kogan Page, London.

Wilkie, W.L. (1986) *Consumer Behaviour*, John Wiley, New York.

Wilkie, W.L. (1990) *Consumer Behaviour*, 2nd edn, John Wiley, New York.

Williams, T.G. (1982) *Consumer Behaviour, Fundamentals and Strategies*, West, Minneapolis/St Paul.

Winer, J. (2000) 'Comment on Leeflang and Wittink', *International Journal of Research in Marketing*, 17, pp. 141–5.

Wolf, M.J. (1999) *The Entertainment Economy*, Penguin, Harmondsworth.

Young, J.H. (1992) *American Health Quackery*, Princeton University Press, Princeton, NJ.

Zaltman, G. and Wallendorf, M. (1983) *Consumer Behaviour. Basic Findings and Management Implications*, 2nd edn, John Wiley, New York.

Zikmund, W.G. and d'Amico, M. (1996) *Effective Marketing: Creating and Keeping Customers*, 5th edn, West, Minneapolis/St Paul.

Zinkhan, G.M. and Herscheim, R. (1992) 'Truth in Marketing Theory and Research: An Alternative Perspective', *Journal of Marketing*, 56 (Spring), pp. 80–8.

Index